You, Your Family, And the Scriptures

You, Your Family, And the Scriptures

Ed J. Pinegar

Deseret Book Company
Salt Lake City, Utah

©1975 Deseret Book Company

All rights reserved. No part of this book may be reproduced in any form or by any means without permission in writing from the publisher, Deseret Book Company, P.O. Box 30178, Salt Lake City, Utah 84130.

Deseret Book is a registered trademark of Deseret Book Company.

First printing in revised edition, August 1990

Library of Congress Catalog Card No. 90-82417
ISBN 0-87579-366-5

Printed in the United States of America

10 9 8 7 6 5 4 3 2 · 1

Contents

Acknowledgments ix
Introduction. xi

PREPARATION

1 Prayer 3
2 Fasting 6
3 The Value of the Standard Works 9
4 The Book of Mormon 13
5 Searching the Scriptures 16
6 Records and Journals. 19
7 Goal Setting. 22

THE DOCTRINE OF CHRIST

8 The Power and Use of Faith 27
9 Faith in Jesus Christ. 30
10 Faith in God 33
11 Repentance 37
12 Forgiveness 40
13 Baptism 43
14 Receiving the Holy Ghost 46
15 Born Again—True Conversion. 49
16 How to Keep the Holy Ghost 52
17 Revelation 55

GOD'S PLAN FOR MAN

18 God Is All-Powerful 61
19 God of Love, Mercy, and Justice 64
20 The Fall 67
21 Temptations 70
22 The Plan of Salvation 73
23 Jesus Christ, Our Savior 77
24 "Come, Follow Me" 80
25 Atonement 83
26 Sacrament 86
27 Resurrection and Judgment 89
28 Our Ultimate Goal: Exaltation 93

GAINING A DIVINE NATURE: CHRISTLIKE ATTRIBUTES

29 Love 99
30 Sacrifice 102
31 Obedience 105
32 Gratitude 108
33 Kindness 111
34 Habits and Traditions 114
35 Attitude 117
36 Courage, Diligence, Endurance 120
37 Courtesy and Manners 123
38 Humility 126
39 Integrity and Sincerity 129
40 Loyalty 132
41 Self-Control 135
42 Self-Esteem 138
43 Tolerance and Patience 141
44 Virtue, Chastity, Modesty 144
45 Envy, Strife, Backbiting, Selfishness, Contention ... 147
46 Criticism and Judging 151
47 Covenant Making and Sustaining Our Leaders ... 154
48 Responsible and Accountable 157
49 Testimony 161

SERVICE AND RESPONSIBILITIES

50 The Priesthood and Its Functions 167
51 Temple Marriage and Endowment.............171
52 The Purpose of Parenthood..................174
53 Family Responsibilities......................177
54 Doing Temple Work 180
55 Tithes and Offerings 183
56 Missionary Work 186
57 The Sabbath Day...........................190
58 Worship and Meditation.....................193

    Observing Special Occasions..................197
    Index......................................199

Acknowledgments

"Our call is for the total membership of the Church to keep the commandments of God, for therein lies the safety of the world." (President Harold B. Lee, general conference address, April 1973.)

People cannot keep the commandments of the Lord until they know what those commandments are. They learn of and about the commandments through searching the scriptures. It is my hope that this book will be of benefit to those who earnestly desire to keep the commandments of God, that each person who reads, studies, and applies the principles herein "will have the Spirit of the Lord to guide him in his individual activities." (Ibid.)

To my wife and family I am indebted for their involvement in our searching of the scriptures. Without their encouragement, this work would never have been undertaken.

A special word of thanks to Beth Marlow, for without her help also this work would not have been possible. Her research, writing, and editing are most appreciated. My thanks also to Eleanor Knowles for her suggestions, encouragement, and skillful editing.

And a most grateful heart for those great prophets who received, by the Spirit, the word of God and recorded it for us, that we might have the opportunity to return to our Heavenly Father.

Introduction

The scriptures show us how to live. They contain the word of God. How do we search the scriptures to find the word of God, to learn how to live? How do we teach our children to search the scriptures, to put them to use in their daily lives? How do we help our family learn that the scriptures are not just "another boring set of books" to read, but are alive and worthwhile and fun—yes, fun—to read and study?

It takes work to search the scriptures. It takes work to teach our children to search the scriptures. Nothing worthwhile in life is easy, and searching the scriptures is no exception. But the Lord will help us. "...for I know that the Lord giveth no commandments unto the children of men, save he shall prepare a way for them that they may accomplish the thing which he commandeth them." (1 Nephi 3:7.)

All we have to do to receive the Lord's help is to ask for it. He has said, "Ask, and it shall be given you; seek, and ye shall find; knock, and it shall be opened unto you: For every one that asketh receiveth; and he that seeketh findeth; and to him that knocketh it shall be opened." (Matthew 7:7–8.)

The Lord has given us the charge to teach our children to search the scriptures; and he will prepare the way for us if we are willing to take the time, if we are willing to seek to understand the scriptures ourselves, if we are willing to ask for help, and if we are willing to see the exciting beauty of the word of God—the power of the word of God. He will help us as Nephi said: "If God had commanded me to do all things I could do them. If he should command me that I should say unto this water, be thou earth, it should be earth; and if I should say it, it would be done." (1 Nephi 17:50.) Yes, God will help us learn to search the scriptures ourselves, and he will help us teach our children to search the scriptures.

The home is where we should search the scriptures and teach our children to do so also. We are to use the scriptures in our daily lives. President Joseph F. Smith said, "The man, and the woman who are the agents, in the providence of God, to bring living souls into the world, are made before God and the heavens, as responsible for these acts as is God himself responsible for the works of his own hands...." (*Gospel Doctrine,* Deseret Book, 18th printing, 1973, p. 273.)

In the Pinegar home, we have felt the need to teach our children the scriptures. After praying, we decided to try the method described in this book. We have used it for more than a year, and now the children ask searching questions more often. Their curiosity has been aroused. Their interest in the scriptures is growing. Family problems are related to the scriptures more frequently than before. The seed has been planted in our children's hearts; we hope it will continue to bear fruit in the future.

Our suggested program is as follows:

1. Topics for scripture study are presented, with a procedure to be used with each one. Each topic is arranged for a week's study and application. Families may choose to select topics at random or they may prefer to go straight through the book as it has been arranged by the author. Reasons for selecting particular subjects will vary from family to family. For example, consider the discussion of prayer. In some families, family prayers may be held regularly but individual prayers may be hurried, without thought, and offered only at night. The chapter on prayer might be chosen to help solve this

problem. Prayer might not be a problem in your family, but you may wish to gain additional insight from the scriptures on this subject. Whatever the reason for selecting a subject or topic, once it has been chosen, a systematic approach for studying the scriptures can begin.

2. Make a bulletin board to help with your systematic scripture study. This may be a chalkboard where things are written and erased, a bulletin board on which items are thumbtacked or pinned, or a piece of paper taped to the wall or refrigerator. On this bulletin board, list the scriptures and purpose for each day. For example, using the subject of prayer, the chart might look like this:

PRAYER

Sunday	Alma 37:36–37	What prayer is
Monday	Mosiah 26:39	Prayer is a commandment
Tuesday	1 Thess. 5:17	When to pray
	D&C 93:49	
	Psalm 55:17	
Wednesday	3 Nephi 19:6	How to pray
	Moroni 10:4	
	D&C 20:47	
Thursday	D&C 19:28	Where to pray
Friday	D&C 46:7	Importance of prayer
Saturday	D&C 9:7–9	Fruits of prayer

Additional scriptures can be found in the Topical Guide in the LDS edition of the Bible under the topics listed at the end of each chapter. These scriptures may be used in combination with, or as substitutes for, those listed each day, whichever the family wishes.

3. On Sunday, read the introduction to the subject of the week. This includes a definition of the subject, a description of its importance, and a statement of the purpose for the week's study of scriptures on the subject. Then read aloud the scriptures suggested for that day. Have family members underline the scriptures in their own copies of the standard works. Discuss each scripture and its application in your family and in

each individual's life. Especially help younger members of the family to understand what each scripture can mean to them.

4. Monday's scripture and application may be used in the family home evening discussion, if the family so desires.

5. Scriptures may be read daily by a family at breakfast or dinner, or they may be read individually and then discussed by the entire family. After the applications are discussed, family members may then individually decide how each will follow through with the applications and make commitments.

6. At the end of each day, each family member may record in his individual journal the scripture for the day, what it means to him, and whether or not he has accomplished the objective for the day. Faith-promoting and other spiritual experiences may also be recorded.

7. At the end of the week, the family can discuss together how they have learned to use the scriptures in their daily life during that week. Then they can select another subject that they will study during the next week.

8. Some persons may wish to use applications different from those listed with each scripture. Other ways to apply the scriptures may include (a) discussing with another person what the scripture means; (b) helping someone else gain a better understanding of what that particular scripture means; (c) praying about it; (d) thinking about it; (e) writing it on a poster or piece of paper and putting it in a prominent place (such as a bathroom mirror or closet door) where it can be pondered upon; (f) writing the scripture on a piece of paper and putting it in a purse or wallet where it can be glanced at and thought about during the day; (g) underlining the scripture in your copy of the standard works; (h) writing out in your own words what the scripture means; (i) finding a hymn about the scripture and singing it or reading the words; (j) memorizing the scripture; (k) reading a paragraph or an article in the *Ensign*, *New Era*, or another Church publication on the subject of the scripture; and (l) putting the principle into action.

You may find that some weeks are more successful than others, and that some days are also more successful than others.

But consistent effort and work can bring satisfaction and great spirituality to the family, as the scriptures come alive and family members begin to use them to help find answers to their problems.

Searching the scriptures can be a fun and most worthwhile family project. The author hopes that this book will be of benefit to your family to help you teach your children to search the scriptures, to help you gain a greater understanding of how the scriptures can be of value in your own life, and to help you take time to really learn from the scriptures and not just read them through and call it done. If you truly search the scriptures, you can come closer to the Lord and your life will be made richer.

Preparation

Prayer

1

Our Heavenly Father has commanded us to pray. Prayer is the vital source of gaining knowledge of him and of learning his will. It gives us strength and helps us solve our problems.

DEFINITION

Prayer is communication with God, as we speak with, thank, ask of, and listen to him.

WHY PRAYER?

"Prayer is a fundamental principle of religion, the Christian religion particularly, and prayer is a force for good. A praying man is a growing man." (David O. McKay, general conference address, April 1929.) Without prayer, one cannot obtain salvation. Prayer is actually communicating with God, talking to him, and listening for his answer. How many times do people do only half of prayer: talking, and refuse to listen to the other half: God's answer? Will we risk our salvation because we have neglected to pray or have made our prayers repetitious sayings that do not rise above the ceiling of our room? The Lord has said we must pray always in mighty prayer. (See Enos 1:4; Alma 6:6; 8:10; 3 Nephi 27:1; D&C 29:2.)

PURPOSE OF THE WEEK

To learn about prayer and to put it into practice in our daily lives.

SUNDAY

Purpose of the day: To learn that prayer is communication with God. (Read Alma 37:36–37.)

Application: We will prepare ourselves when we pray; get in the proper attitude; really talk to God and then listen for his answer; and read what the scriptures have to say about prayer, especially D&C 88:63–64 and Moses 5:8.

MONDAY

Purpose of the day: To learn that God has commanded everyone to pray. (Read Mosiah 26:39.)

Application: We will discuss prayer in all its aspects with our family. Hymn 145, "Prayer Is the Soul's Sincere Desire," or another favorite hymn about prayer can aid the discussion.

TUESDAY

Purpose of the day: To learn when to pray. (Read D&C 93:49; Psalm 55:17; 3 Nephi 20:1.)

Application: We will look up in the dictionary what the words *always* and *continuous* mean, write down how they apply to prayer, and then begin to apply them in our lives. (See Alma 34:17–28.)

WEDNESDAY

Purpose of the day: To learn how to pray. (Read Moroni 10:4; D&C 20:47.)

Application: In our prayers, do we just say a few words and leave it at that, or do we pour out our soul like Enos, having faith in Jesus Christ? Can we think a prayer when we can't get down on our knees? (Victor Hugo said, "There are moments when, whatever be the attitude of the body, the soul is on its knees.") We will be an "Enos" for a day: pray all day and into the night. Then we will read the Book of Enos. (Read also 2 Nephi 33:12 and Matthew 6:5–8.)

THURSDAY

Purpose of the day: To learn where to pray. (Read D&C 19:28.)
Application: We will pray in many different places so as to realize the necessity of praying always.

FRIDAY

Purpose of the day: To learn what to pray for. (Read D&C 46:7.)
Application: What are some important things to consider in prayer? (1) God's purposes will be fulfilled—Matthew 6:10; (2) We will know his will—D&C 50:29–30; (3) We will receive answers to questions—D&C 9:7–9; and (4) We will receive help in all things—Alma 34:17–27. We will pray for Heavenly Father's purposes so that our will may be like his will. (Read Helaman 10:4–5.)

SATURDAY

Purpose of the day: To learn of the personal fruits of prayer. (Read D&C 88:63–64.)
Application: Are we happy that the Lord answers prayers, that he heals people, that he guides us, that he will give us spiritual gifts through the Holy Ghost, that he will draw near to us? Are we willing to put prayer to the test? God will do as he has promised. (Read 3 Nephi 24:10.) We will make prayer an important part of our lives from this day forward.

For additional scriptures see Topical Guide, "Prayer."

Fasting

2

"Fasting originated when the Lord first revealed to man the gospel plan, thus antedating even the law of Moses, when an annual fast day was prescribed (see Lev. 23:27–29)." (David O. McKay, Millennial Star, *84:424.)*

DEFINITION

Fasting means abstaining from food and/or drink for a period of time, with a religious purpose in mind.

WHY FASTING?

Fasting, with prayer, is the very key to obtaining faith and humility and gaining the power of God. (See Helaman 3:35; Alma 17:2–3.) With this faith, humility, and power, we realize our dependence upon God; we also increase our own self-control and improve our health.

PURPOSE OF THE WEEK

To learn about fasting and to put it into practice in our lives.

Preparation

SUNDAY

Purpose of the day: To learn that fasting is a commandment of the Lord. (Read D&C 88:76.)

Application: We will write down reasons why we feel that fasting, along with prayer, is important enough to be a commandment of God, and then read these scriptures on fasting: 2 Samuel 12:16; Isaiah 58:1–12; Matthew 6:16–18; Alma 6:6; Moroni 6:5; D&C 59:14–16.

MONDAY

Purpose of the day: To learn how to fast. (Read 3 Nephi 13:16–18.)

Application: Church practice is for each person to fast for two meals once a month and to donate the cost of the two meals to the fast offering fund to help those who are less fortunate. By such prayerful sacrifice, great personal benefits can be derived. Individuals may also fast at other times when they feel the need. (The Lord has said that wisdom is to be used in fasting, for those whose health problems do not allow them to make a complete fast.) We will discuss fasting and how to do it with members of our family. (Compare Matthew 6:16–18; 3 Nephi 13:16–18.) Hymn 219, "Because I Have Been Given Much," can reinforce the discussion.

TUESDAY

Purpose of the day: To learn to seek and serve God through fasting. (Read Daniel 9:3.)

Application: By abstaining from food and drink for a period of time and thus gaining control over our natural selves and letting our spiritual selves gain ascendance, we can get spiritually closer to the Lord and improve our service to him. We will conduct a special personal fast, with humble prayer, in order that we might thus draw closer to the Lord.

WEDNESDAY

Purpose of the day: To learn humility through fasting. (Read Psalm 35:13.)

Application: The Lord cannot work through those who are self-righteous, hypocritical, or who think they know it all. He works through those who are humble and willing to learn. We will write down how fasting can help us become more humble and then put this into practice in our lives.

THURSDAY

Purpose of the day: To learn truths and gain a testimony through fasting. (Read Alma 5:46.)

Application: The next time we wish to know the truth of something, we will read Alma 5:46 and Moroni 10:4–5 and will follow the counsel given therein.

FRIDAY

Purpose of the day: To learn that fasting can help us become instruments in the hands of the Lord. (Read Alma 17:9.)

Application: We will fast and pray in order that we might know what the Lord wants us to do.

SATURDAY

Purpose of the day: To learn that fasting leads to sanctification. (Read Helaman 3:35.)

Application: Through fasting, we learn self-mastery and can overcome the natural man as we yield to the enticings of the Holy Spirit. We will write down how fasting can help us personally gain sanctification.

For additional scriptures see Topical Guide, "Fast, Fasting."

The Value of the Standard Works

3

"They [the scriptures] are intended to enlarge man's spiritual endowments and to reveal and intensify the bond of relationship between him and his God." (Joseph F. Smith, Instructor, 47:204.)

DEFINITION

The scriptures are sacred, holy writings or documents. They include the Old and New Testaments (the Bible), the Book of Mormon, the Doctrine and Covenants, and the Pearl of Great Price. In addition, scripture is described in modern revelation as that which is spoken under the influence of the Holy Ghost. (D&C 68:4.)

WHY ARE THE SCRIPTURES OF VALUE?

The scriptures, given for the benefit of man, teach the gospel and help us gain a testimony of its truth. In order to appreciate and learn from these sacred writings, they "must be studied by those spiritually inclined and who are in quest of spiritual truths." (Joseph F. Smith, *Instructor*, vol. 47, p. 204.) After all, the scriptures are to teach, inspire, and help those who use them, and, indeed, they are to condemn those who will not use them in their lives. (See D&C 42:60.) If people will but feast upon the scriptures and delight in them, they will know all things they should do in life. (See 2 Nephi 32:3 and 2 Nephi 4:15.)

PURPOSE OF THE WEEK

To learn the real value of the scriptures and to begin putting those values into our daily lives.

SUNDAY

Purpose of the day: To learn that the scriptures give examples for us to follow, for our own admonition. (Read 1 Corinthians 10:11.)

Application: Do we see and understand the value of searching the scriptures for the examples, experiences, and teachings of the prophets? In this way, we may learn vicariously without personally experiencing sin. We will read the following scriptures, which discuss example: 1 Corinthians 10:1–12; 1 Nephi 19:23; 2 Nephi 31:9, 16; Alma 17:11; Mormon 7:10; D&C 58:35; D&C 88:130–31. Then we will write down our favorite example in the scriptures and read the scripture that describes it.

MONDAY

Purpose of the day: To learn that the scriptures explain that all must take on Christ's name (including his church). (Read 3 Nephi 27:5.)

Application: In addition to telling us to take Christ's name upon ourselves, the scriptures also testify of Christ (see John 5:39; Jacob 7:10–11; Alma 21:9) and are a witness to the divinity of Christ and to all the works and words of the Lord (see Alma 34:30). With our family, we will discuss how the scriptures testify of Christ. Hymns 271, "Oh, Holy Words of Truth and

Love"; 274, "The Iron Rod"; and 277, "As I Search the Holy Scriptures," can reinforce this concept.

TUESDAY

Purpose of the day: To learn that the scriptures reveal the gospel. (Read D&C 42:12.)
Application: Do we know what the gospel is? Can we define it, live it, follow its precepts, principles, and teachings? We must study the scriptures in order to learn about the gospel. (See Helaman 15:7; D&C 76:40ff; 3 Nephi 27:8–13; 19–21.) We will read and ponder the ninth Article of Faith.

WEDNESDAY

Purpose of the day: To learn that the scriptures contain the truths of God, which are endless. (Read D&C 1:37–39.)
Application: We will read and ponder the eighth Article of Faith.

THURSDAY

Purpose of the day: To learn that the scriptures are given for the instruction of the people. (Read 2 Timothy 3:16–17.)
Application: The leaders of the Church quote the scriptures extensively in their talks. Can we learn from the scriptures and live by them? We will write down in one brief sentence how we can learn from the scriptures.

FRIDAY

Purpose of the day: To learn that the scriptures contain the laws of God given to govern the people and that they will help us to live with him once more. (Read D&C 42:59–60.)
Application: We will write down the two great commandments (Matthew 22:36–40) and evaluate ourselves as to our present status in regard to those commandments.

SATURDAY

Purpose of the day: To learn that we will be judged out of the books of scripture, whether or not we have followed the laws and commandments given in them. (Read 2 Nephi 29:11.)
Application: We will make a list of the commandments in the scriptures and then work on them one at a time.

For additional scriptures see Topical Guide, "Scriptures, Study of"; "Scriptures, Value of."

The Book of Mormon

4

"I told the brethren that the Book of Mormon was the most correct of any book on earth, and the keystone of our religion, and a man would get nearer to God by abiding its precepts, than by any other book." (Joseph Smith, History of the Church, 4:461.)

Because the Book of Mormon contains the fulness of the gospel and is a witness of Christ, it can help convert and teach people how to obey and follow the teachings of the Lord. Those who abide by its precepts, according to the prophets, will return to live with their Father in heaven in the life after this one. However, "The book of Mormon does not in any degree conflict with or take the place of the Holy Bible, but is the strongest corroborative evidence in existence of the divine origin of that sacred record." (Statement of the First Presidency, in *Liahona*, April 15, 1930 [vol. 27], p. 512.)

PURPOSE OF THE WEEK

To learn about the Book of Mormon and its purpose and value in our lives.

SUNDAY

Purpose of the day: To learn that the Book of Mormon can help convince people that Jesus is the Christ. (Read 1 Nephi 13:40.) Also, to learn that it was written to convince "the Jew and Gentile that Jesus is the Christ, the Eternal God, manifesting himself unto all nations...." (Introduction to the Book of Mormon.)

Application: We will read the following scriptures in the Book of Mormon about Christ being the Savior of the world, which will help increase our testimonies: 1 Nephi 10:4; 1 Nephi 22:12; 3 Nephi 5:20; Mormon 7:10; Moroni 8:8.

MONDAY

Purpose of the day: To learn that the Book of Mormon, together with the Bible, contains a testimony of the Lord. (Read Mormon 7:8–9.)

Application: We will see that each member of our family over eight years of age has his own copy of each of the standard works, and we will discuss the fact that the Book of Mormon is a witness to the Bible. Hymns 13, "An Angel from on High," and 274, "The Iron Rod," can enhance this discussion.

TUESDAY

Purpose of the day: To learn that the Book of Mormon was written to convince the Lamanites that they are of the House of Israel. (Read Mormon 5:12.)

Application: We will write down how this purpose for the Book of Mormon is important in our own lives.

WEDNESDAY

Purpose of the day: To learn that the Book of Mormon restores many plain and precious truths and contains the fulness of the gospel. (Read D&C 20:8–9; 1 Nephi 13:34.)

Application: We will list two things found in the Book of Mormon that were lost or distorted and that are now clear.

THURSDAY

Purpose of the day: To learn that the Book of Mormon was written to convince mankind that each person will be judged for his own works. (Read Mormon 3:20–22.)

Application: Are we prepared to meet Christ? Are we willing to read the Book of Mormon to learn what we must do to face the Lord at the judgment seat? We will begin a systematic study of the Book of Mormon so that we might learn what we must do to face the Lord at the last day.

FRIDAY

Purpose of the day: To learn that the Book of Mormon can help people of our own generation solve their problems. (Read Mormon 8:34–35.)

Application: We will each list a problem we have that teachings in the Book of Mormon can help us solve, and we will begin to work on solving our problems.

SATURDAY

Purpose of the day: To learn to follow the admonition of Moroni and receive a testimony of the truth of the Book of Mormon. (Read Moroni 10:4.)

Application: We will get down on our knees and ask the Lord if the Book of Mormon is true.

For additional scriptures see Topical Guide, "Book of Mormon."

Searching the Scriptures

5

"Search the Scriptures—search the revelations which we publish and ask your Heavenly Father, in the name of His Son Jesus Christ, to manifest the truth unto you, and if you do it with an eye single to His glory, nothing doubting, He will answer you by the power of His Holy Spirit. You will then know for yourselves and not for another." (Joseph Smith, History of the Church, *1:282.)*

DEFINITION
Search means to explore, to examine, to seek. It includes inquiry, investigation, probing, questing, penetrating, endeavoring to find, and ascertaining.

WHY SEARCH THE SCRIPTURES?
The main reason to search the scriptures is to gain salvation and exaltation. Through searching the scriptures we can learn of God, his ways, his laws, his precepts, and what he wants us to do. "Would it not be wise for the members of the Church to pay more heed to these counsels...?" (Joseph Fielding

Smith, *Answers to Gospel Questions,* Deseret Book, 1958, vol. 2, p. 205.)

PURPOSE OF THE WEEK
To begin a systematic study of the scriptures so that we may use them in our daily lives.

SUNDAY
Purpose of the day: To search the scriptures to learn of God and his ways. (Read Alma 30:44.)
Application: The need to know God is vital to our eternal progression. We will begin to learn of him through searching the scriptures and using prayer. We will also read these scriptures that tell of God: 1 Corinthians 14:33; 2 Nephi 2:21; D&C 1:1–2; Moses 1:2–3.

MONDAY
Purpose of the day: To develop the habit of searching the scriptures every day. (Read Acts 17:11.)
Application: With our family, we will discuss how to search the scriptures and will set up a daily schedule to do so. Hymn 274, "The Iron Rod," may help reinforce the application of this purpose.

TUESDAY
Purpose of the day: To search the scriptures for our own profit and learning. (Read 1 Nephi 19:23.)
Application: We will write down two things we want to gain, for our profit and learning, from searching the scriptures.

WEDNESDAY
Purpose of the day: To search the scriptures diligently. (Read Alma 17:2.)
Application: We will write out the definition of the word *diligently* in relation to searching the scriptures. We will then

read Alma 17:2–4 and see what happened when the people searched the scriptures diligently.

THURSDAY

Purpose of the day: To search the scriptures in order to gain eternal life. (Read John 5:39.)
Application: We will write down how the scriptures can help us to gain eternal life.

FRIDAY

Purpose of the day: To search the scriptures to learn about the prophecies that have been and are to be fulfilled. (Read 3 Nephi 10:11.)
Application: We will write down at least one prophecy that we know has been fulfilled and where that prophecy is found in the scriptures.

SATURDAY

Purpose of the day: To begin, as a child, to search the scriptures, and to teach our children to do so. (Read 2 Timothy 3:15.)
Application: We will evaluate our schedule for searching the scriptures as we have followed it this past week. If changes are needed, we will make them. We will continue in the future to search the scriptures diligently and daily.

For additional scriptures see Topical Guide, "Scriptures, Study of."

Records and Journals
6

We should each keep individual and family records of material that pertains to our own welfare and that may be of benefit to others in their quest for eternal life.

DEFINITION
A journal is a record, a diary, an account of certain events. It should be written in daily or systematically whenever special events occur.

WHY RECORDS AND JOURNALS?
The Lord has made record keeping important from the beginning of the world, when he commanded Adam to keep a record of himself, his family, and the things of importance in his day and age. This commandment has been reiterated down through the ages. Not only is it important for each person to keep a record of the important events in his or her life, but it is also important to keep a record of the family, especially from a genealogical standpoint, for without accurate records, vicarious work for the dead cannot be performed.

PURPOSE OF THE WEEK

To learn the importance of keeping records and to help us begin keeping accurate records of those things that are important to us and for our posterity.

SUNDAY

Purpose of the day: To learn that the Lord has commanded his people to keep records. (Read Mosiah 28:20; D&C 21:1.)
Application: Do we know where all the documents and important papers pertaining to the welfare of ourselves and of our family are located? We will bring our records up to date and organize important papers and documents for safekeeping. Reading the following scriptures will help us to apply this commandment: Nehemiah 7:5; Revelation 1:1–3; Alma 37:2; D&C 6:26; 85:1.

MONDAY

Purpose of the day: To write down those things which are worthwhile. (Read 1 Nephi 6:6.)
Application: We will discuss with our family the importance of making and preserving the important things of life in records and journals and challenge them to begin keeping their own journals and records. Hymn 226, "Improve the Shining Moments," can aid with this concept.

TUESDAY

Purpose of the day: To learn that the Church has been commanded to keep records. (Read D&C 47:3.)
Application: We will make an appointment with our ward or branch clerk to ascertain that our own membership records are accurate and up to date.

WEDNESDAY

Purpose of the day: To learn that we will be judged out of the records that are written. (Read 3 Nephi 27:25.)

Application: What kind of life will our journals reflect? We will read Ezra 2:61–62 and Nehemiah 7:63–64 about people who were wicked and had their names blotted from the records of the church. We will also read Revelation 20:12.

THURSDAY

Purpose of the day: To learn of past generations from the records they have left behind. (Read Moses 6:45–46.)

Application: We will try to locate a journal or record of one of our ancestors so that we may read about this person and learn from his or her experiences.

FRIDAY

Purpose of the day: To understand that our own posterity can learn of us from the records and journals we keep. (Read Abraham 1:31.)

Application: We will write down the things that we would like our posterity to learn from us and to remember us by, and will prepare an outline or checklist for keeping our own records or journals up to date.

SATURDAY

Purpose of the day: To make sure our records are in order. (Read D&C 127:9.)

Application: We will begin an orderly process of record making and keeping. If necessary, we will sort out the important records and items we are keeping and put them in our journals or records. We will resolve to continue keeping orderly records.

For additional scriptures see Topical Guide, "Record Keeping."

Goal Setting

7

Without a plan or objective in life, chaos can result. We cannot be spiritually in tune unless we are in control of our own lives and have high goals and objectives toward which we will work.

DEFINITION
Goals are those objectives toward which a person aims his life, his work, and/or his activities.

WHY GOAL SETTING?
Without setting goals or objectives in life, a person's activities can be aimless and achievements doubtful. It is through setting goals and working toward them that life becomes worthwhile. "We use so much of our time in rushing around, not thinking always what we ought to be, nor what it is that matters most. Sometimes we set our hearts on things we feel we have to have, and when we get them find they don't mean as much as once we thought they would." (Richard L. Evans, general conference address, April 1971.) The most important goal is that of exaltation in the celestial kingdom, toward which all other goals are but stepping stones.

PURPOSE OF THE WEEK

To set the goal of exaltation and those attendant goals that will help us achieve it.

SUNDAY

Purpose of the day: To have the desire to achieve our goals. (Read Proverbs 11:23.)
Application: We will write down why desire is necessary to achieve a worthwhile goal and will read these scriptures about desire: Alma 32:21–43; 3 Nephi 28:29; D&C 6:8; 11:10.

MONDAY

Purpose of the day: To learn that the Savior says we must prepare ourselves (or set goals). (Read D&C 50:46.)
Application: We will discuss with our family the setting of goals and achieving them, stressing the importance that the Savior has placed on our doing so. Hymns 30, "Come, Come, Ye Saints," and 116, "Come, Follow Me," may be of benefit to the discussion.

TUESDAY

Purpose of the day: To plan our goals following self-evaluation. (Read 2 Corinthians 13:5; D&C 88:74; Proverbs 20:18.)
Application: Before we can set appropriate goals in our lives, we must evaluate ourselves. Then we can determine which goals we need to set in order to attain eternal life and exaltation. We will evaluate ourselves and then set down some goals we want to achieve as well as ways to achieve them. (See Alma 5.)

WEDNESDAY

Purpose of the day: To recognize the need for short-term and long-term goals. (Read D&C 58:26–27.)
Application: Achieving success in short-term goals can enhance our attitude toward goals and help us in achieving those that

are long-term. We will categorize our goals into short-term and long-term goals and then list all the short-term goals that support the long-term goals.

THURSDAY

Purpose of the day: To begin to work toward achieving our goals. (Read D&C 18:38; 42:42.)
Application: We will write out the steps we must take to achieve one or more of the goals we have set.

FRIDAY

Purpose of the day: To begin to make our goals viable in our lives. (Read Isaiah 56:4.)
Application: We will make a timetable for achieving our goals so we can see where we are going.

SATURDAY

Purpose of the day: To understand that the Lord will help us achieve our goals. (Read Alma 29:4–5.)
Application: We will ask the Lord for specific help with one or more of the goals we have set.

For additional scriptures see Topical Guide, "Objectives"; "Perfection."

The Doctrine of Christ

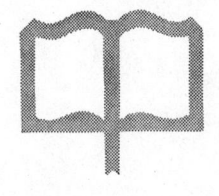

The Power and Use of Faith

8

Faith is "the first great governing principle, which has power, dominion and authority over all things." (Joseph Smith, Lecture on Faith 1.)

DEFINITION
"Now faith is the substance of things hoped for, the evidence of things not seen." (Hebrews 11:1.)

WHY THE POWER AND USE OF FAITH?
If faith is not used for good works, faith is dead; it cannot live. Joseph Smith said that "faith is the principle of action and of power in all intelligent beings, both in heaven and on earth...; for it is by faith that the Deity works.... We understand that when a man works by faith he works by mental exertion instead of physical force; it is by words instead of exerting his physical powers, with which every being works when he works by faith." (*Lecture on Faith*, no. 7.)

PURPOSE OF THE WEEK

To learn the power and use of faith and how to put it to work in our lives.

SUNDAY

Purpose of the day: To learn that we can do any righteous thing by faith. (Read Moroni 10:23; 1 Nephi 3:7.)
Application: We will list two things that we know have been accomplished by faith. We will also read these scriptures: Ether 12:3; D&C 8:10; 18:19; Mark 9:23; Galatians 5:6.

MONDAY

Purpose of the day: To learn that prayers are answered according to the faith exercised. (Read Moroni 7:26.)
Application: We will discuss the power and use of faith with our family, especially regarding the answering of prayers. Hymns 180, "Father in Heaven, We Do Believe," and 285, "God Moves in a Mysterious Way," may help reinforce the discussion.

TUESDAY

Purpose of the day: To learn that all knowledge is received through faith and study. (Read D&C 88:118.)
Application: We will write down something that we need to know that will be beneficial to us in life. We will then study and pray with faith and will listen for the promptings of the Holy Spirit.

WEDNESDAY

Purpose of the day: To learn that miracles are wrought by faith. (Read Ether 12:16, 18.)
Application: Faith is the avenue that brings miracles to pass. We will write down a miracle we have seen or heard about or read about, and then write down whose faith brought it about. We will read 3 Nephi 8:1, on personal preparation for receiving miracles.

THURSDAY

Purpose of the day: To learn that the power of faith can move mountains. (Read Jacob 4:6; Matthew 17:20.)
Application: We will write down the steps we need to go through to attain greater faith in God and his Son, Jesus Christ.

FRIDAY

Purpose of the day: To learn that faith can be used to heal the sick and afflicted. (Read D&C 42:48–51.)
Application: If we or one of our loved ones have ever been healed by faith, we will write a letter of thanks to that person whose faith helped heal us and will also acknowledge God, who is the giver of all things.

SATURDAY

Purpose of the day: To learn that God works with men through their faith. (See 2 Nephi 27:23.)
Application: Faith dwells independently in God, and members of the priesthood act by the power of faith as moved upon by the Holy Ghost. We will write down when and for what we would like the Lord's help or what we can do to bless someone in our life. Then, with faith, we will ask for that help and guidance.

For additional scriptures see Topical Guide, "Faith"; "Faithful."

Faith in Jesus Christ
9

"Faith being the first principle in revealed religion, and the foundation of all righteousness, necessarily claims the first place in a course of lectures which are designed to unfold to the understanding the doctrine of Jesus Christ." (Joseph Smith, Lecture on Faith 1.)

DEFINITION

Faith in Christ means believing in him, trusting him, and following his commandments. It includes following his precepts and his example.

WHY FAITH IN CHRIST?

Without faith in Christ, we cannot follow his teachings or obey his commandments. Faith in Christ brings about a positive response or reaction to what he wants done. "It means," according to President David O. McKay, "that we accept Jesus Christ, not merely as a great teacher, a powerful leader, but as the Savior, the Redeemer of the world.... I would have all men keep that faith. I think it is fundamental to man's happiness, fundamental to his peace of mind. I think it is the cardinal principle of the Church of Jesus Christ." (General conference address, October 1928.)

PURPOSE OF THE WEEK

To increase our faith in the Lord Jesus Christ.

SUNDAY

Purpose of the day: To learn that faith in Christ is necessary in all things. (Read Enos 1:15.)
Application: The Lord has said that faith in Christ should be a part of our daily lives. We will write down why faith in Christ is necessary in our lives. We will also read these scriptures on faith in Christ: John 3:14–18; Galatians 2:20; 1 Nephi 12:10; Enos 1:8; D&C 29:42; 68:25.

MONDAY

Purpose of the day: To understand better the fact that everyone must learn to have faith in Christ. (Read D&C 68:25.)
Application: We will discuss faith in Jesus Christ with members of our family and how it can help our lives become better, richer, and fuller, and help us to return to our Heavenly Father's presence. Hymn 258, "O Thou Rock of Our Salvation," can assist the discussion.

TUESDAY

Purpose of the day: To learn that salvation comes through faith in Jesus Christ. (Read D&C 33:12.)
Application: We will write down the steps to salvation that we must achieve and put faith as the number one step in our list. We will review this list periodically to check our progress.

WEDNESDAY

Purpose of the day: To learn that peace of mind comes from faith in Christ. (Read Mosiah 4:3.)

Application: We will make a commitment to the Lord that we will strive to give his peace to others through teaching faith in Christ and through living his commandments.

THURSDAY

Purpose of the day: To learn truth through faith in Jesus Christ. (Read Moroni 10:4.)
Application: We will write down one truth for which we are searching and will ask the Lord, in faith.

FRIDAY

Purpose of the day: To learn that good comes from living by faith in Jesus Christ. (Read Moroni 7:21, 25.)
Application: We will list at least two good things that we have received because of living by faith in Jesus Christ.

SATURDAY

Purpose of the day: To learn that such blessings as baptism, repentance, the gift of the Holy Ghost, and the power to do all things come from and through faith in Jesus Christ. (Read Mormon 9:37.)
Application: We will write down two blessings we have already received through faith in the Lord Jesus Christ, and then one blessing that we would like to receive. We will strive to make our faith stronger so that we might receive this blessing.

For additional scriptures see Topical Guide, "Faith"; "Faithfulness."

Faith in God

10

In order to show our great love for God, we must have faith in him and exercise the privilege of prayer, fasting, and obedience to all other commandments.

DEFINITION

Faith in God means believing in him, trusting him, being true to our promises to him, being loyal to him, and giving him our complete confidence. It also includes allegiance to him in all things.

WHY FAITH IN GOD?

Faith in God produces an understanding of what he is like, why he has put us here on earth, and why we are his children. It precludes the fact that we are created in his image and that we may become as he is. It produces action. Joseph Smith said, "It is the first principle of the Gospel to know for a certainty the Character of God, and to know that we may converse with him as one man converses with another, and that he was once a man like us...." (*Teachings of the Prophet Joseph Smith,* pp. 345–46.)

PURPOSE OF THE WEEK

To understand faith in God and to put it into action in our lives.

SUNDAY

Purpose of the day: To learn what faith is and to apply it in our lives. (Read Hebrews 11:1.)

Application: We will read the following statement from the Prophet Joseph Smith and discuss with our family how it applies in our lives: "... faith is the assurance which men have of the existence of things which they have not seen; and the principle of action in all intelligent beings.... Faith, then, is the first great governing principle which has power, dominion, and authority over all things; by it they exist, by it they are upheld, by it they are changed, or by it they remain, agreeably to the will of God. Without it, there is no power, and without power there could be no creation, nor existence." (Lecture on Faith, no. 1.) We will also read Alma 32:21–27; Ether 12:6; Ephesians 2:8–9; and John 3:16 to learn more about faith.

MONDAY

Purpose of the day: To learn that faith in God can come only after we have learned about and gained knowledge of God. (Read John 17:3.)

Application: We will discuss with our family the nature of God. The following quotations may be helpful in the discussion: "... you have come here [on earth] to get a practical experience and to learn yourselves. You will then begin to learn more perfectly the things of God. No being can thoroughly know himself, without understanding more or less of the things of God...." (Brigham Young, *Journal of Discourses*, vol. 8, p. 334.) "... we are the children of God. He is the Father of our spirits... and we belong to the royal family, because he is our Father." (George Albert Smith, general conference address, April 1946.) We will also read and discuss Romans

8:16–17. Hymn 62, "All Creatures of Our God and King," can add to the discussion.

TUESDAY

Purpose of the day: To learn that faith in God is a commandment. (Read Mark 11:22.)
Application: We will list all the blessings that come from this commandment.

WEDNESDAY

Purpose of the day: We will learn that even though we work for it, faith in God is a gift from God. (Read Moroni 10:11.)
Application: We will write down why we feel that faith is a gift from God, even though we must work for it.

THURSDAY

Purpose of the day: To learn that the glories of God's creations can help us increase our faith in him. (Read Alma 30:44.)
Application: The Prophet Joseph Smith said: "... the things of God are of deep import; and time, and experience, and careful and ponderous and solemn thoughts can only find them out. Thy mind, O man! if thou wilt lead a soul unto salvation, must stretch as high as the utmost heavens, and search into and contemplate the darkest abyss, and the broad expanse of eternity—thou must commune with God." (*Teachings of the Prophet Joseph Smith,* p. 137.) We will look at some of the creations of God, such as a flower, a tree, a butterfly, a blade of grass, the heavens, and think about these creations and the wonder of them. We will then read Abraham 3 and Hebrews 11:3.

FRIDAY

Purpose of the day: To learn that faith in God can increase a person's intelligence and knowledge. (Read D&C 50:24.)
Application: We will choose a true law of science and then see how it fits in with God's laws and is part of his plan. We will read D&C 88:118.

SATURDAY

Purpose of the day: To learn that God will hear and answer the prayers of faith. (Read 2 Nephi 33:3.)
Application: We will evaluate our actions to see if knowledge and faith in God are reflected in our lives.

For additional scriptures see Topical Guide, "Faith"; "Faithfulness."

Repentance

11

"In your soul-searching, if you seek for and you find... peace of conscience, by that token you may know that the Lord has accepted of your repentance." (Harold B. Lee, general conference address, April 1973.)

DEFINITION

Repentance means to change our mind, our actions, or our conduct with regard to past actions. It includes regret for past actions and/or behavior, and cleansing ourselves from these things through Jesus Christ, our Savior.

WHY REPENTANCE?

Repentance and coming to Christ is the major message of all scripture. It is the first step, following faith, on the path toward eternal life and exaltation. Without repentance, we cannot gain salvation nor live with our Heavenly Father, for "no unclean thing can dwell with God." (1 Nephi 10:21.) Our repentance must also be real and not just lip service. "Repentance without amendment is like continually pumping without mending the leak." (Lewis W. Dilwyn.) "Repentance is a hearty sorrow for our past misdeeds, and is a sincere resolution and endeavor, to the utmost of our power, to conform all our actions to the law of God. It does not consist in one single act of sorrow, but in doing works meet for repentance; in a sincere obedience to the law of Christ for the remainder of our lives." (John Locke.)

PURPOSE OF THE WEEK
To become a more repentant person.

SUNDAY
Purpose of the day: To learn that repentance is a commandment of God. (Read 2 Nephi 2:21.)
Application: Each member of the family will list at least three things of which he or she needs to repent and will check on his or her progress periodically. We will read the following scriptures on repentance: Isaiah 55:6–7; 1 John 1:9; D&C 1:31–32; 58:43; 64:7, 9–10; 93:1.

MONDAY
Purpose of the day: To learn that we must be sincere in our repentance. (Read Mosiah 4:10.)
Application: We will discuss the meaning of sincere repentance with our family. Hymns 117, "Come Unto Jesus," and 157, "Thy Spirit, Lord, Has Stirred Our Souls," can reinforce the discussion.

TUESDAY
Purpose of the day: To learn that Jesus suffered that we might not have to—if we repent. (Read D&C 18:11–13.)
Application: We will thank our Father in heaven in prayer that Christ suffered and atoned for us, and we will promise to repent that we might not also have to suffer.

WEDNESDAY

Purpose of the day: To learn that one cannot be saved in sin. (Read Helaman 5:10–11.)
Application: We will check up on how we are progressing in our repentance begun on Sunday and will read the words of Amulek in Alma 11:34–37.

THURSDAY

Purpose of the day: To learn the several steps to repentance. (Read Acts 2:37–38.)
Application: Repentance can only come following that "pricked heart," which is the actual realization that we have committed a sin (or more than one, as the case may be). Leaders of the Church have given the following steps for achieving true repentance: (1) recognizing that we have sinned, (2) feeling regret, remorse, contrition, godly sorrow for what we have done, (3) asking for forgiveness, (4) refraining from sin in the future (becoming obedient to the laws and commandments of God), and (5) making restitution wherever and whenever possible. We will follow these five steps in repenting of a specific sin we have committed.

FRIDAY

Purpose of the day: To realize that problems arise when we procrastinate repentance. (Read Alma 34:35.)
Application: We will commit ourselves to repentance for the rest of our lives, that we may not be in Satan's power, but that we may one day come into the presence of our Father in Heaven.

SATURDAY

Purpose of the day: To learn that when we sincerely and truly repent, the Lord will forget that we have ever sinned. (Read D&C 58:42.)
Application: We will recheck our progress in the repenting that we began on Sunday.

For additional scriptures see Topical Guide, "Repent."

Forgiveness

12

"The miracle of forgiveness is available to all of those who turn from their evil doings and return no more...." *(Harold B. Lee, general conference, April 1973.)*

DEFINITION
Forgiveness means to pardon, to stop resenting something or someone because of a past offense. It means there will be no revenge or retaliation.

WHY FORGIVENESS?
"To err is human; to forgive, divine." (Alexander Pope.) The Lord requires us to forgive others, and without forgiveness, we cannot be forgiven. It is closely allied with repentance. "A wise man will make haste to forgive, because he knows the full value of time and will not suffer it to pass away in unnecessary pain." (Rambler.) When we forgive another person, we have a good feeling inside; we feel as if a burden has been lifted from our soul. And when we receive forgiveness, another burden has also been lifted.

PURPOSE OF THE WEEK

To become a more forgiving person and to use and ask for forgiveness in our lives.

SUNDAY

Purpose of the day: To learn that forgiveness comes following repentance and obedience. (Read D&C 1:32.)

Application: Each of us will write down a wrong of which we have repented and will evaluate our lives to see if the Lord has forgiven us. We will read these additional scriptures on forgiveness: 1 Kings 8:39; Psalm 103:1–13; Ephesians 4:32, Enos 5; Mosiah 4:10.

MONDAY

Purpose of the day: To learn that the Lord requires us to forgive others. (Read D&C 64:9–10.)

Application: We will discuss with our family the importance of forgiving others. We will tell members of our family that we forgive each one for anything (little or great) they might have done to offend us. Hymn 95, "Now Thank We All Our God," can reinforce the concept of forgiveness.

TUESDAY

Purpose of the day: To learn that we must forgive every time it is asked of us, not just the first time. (Read Matthew 18:21–22.)

Application: We will make a commitment to forgive everyone, every time they ask for it (or even if they don't ask for it), whenever they have done something wrong.

WEDNESDAY

Purpose of the day: To learn that condemnation comes if we don't forgive others. (Read Mosiah 26:31.)

Application: We will write down what will happen to us specifically if we don't forgive others: our own personal condemnation.

THURSDAY

Purpose of the day: To learn that we must *ask* to receive forgiveness from the Lord. (Read Moroni 6:8.)
Application: We will ask the Lord for forgiveness of a specific wrong or sin or iniquity that we have committed and then repented of.

FRIDAY

Purpose of the day: To learn that forgiveness follows the "Golden Rule." (Read D&C 82:1.)
Application: We will forgive someone who is near and dear to us and ask for forgiveness from someone for whom we care; then compare 3 Nephi 13:14–15 with Matthew 6:14–15.

SATURDAY

Purpose of the day: To learn that we must change our lives after repenting and being forgiven. (Read Ether 2:15.)
Application: We will make a commitment to the Lord that we will change our lives for the better from this point on. The Lord will forgive us our trespasses and bless us for doing it.

For additional scriptures see Topical Guide, "Forgive."

Baptism

13

Baptism is a principle and an ordinance of the gospel, and a symbol of a covenant made with God. We take the name of Christ upon us through this holy act.

DEFINITION
Baptism usually means to immerse in water as a religious rite. It includes the idea of cleansing and purifying. Baptism is a covenant between God and man.

WHY BAPTISM?
Baptism is necessary for several reasons: (1) to wash away sin, (2) to gain membership in The Church of Jesus Christ of Latter-day Saints, the kingdom of God on earth, (3) to take the first step on the straight and narrow path that leads to eternal life in the celestial kingdom, (4) to promise to bear one another's burdens, (5) to take upon ourselves the name of Christ, and (6) to begin our personal sanctification. (See 3 Nephi 27:20.)

PURPOSE OF THE WEEK

To understand baptism and the covenants made therein so we may keep our part of the covenant.

SUNDAY

Purpose of the day: To learn that baptism is a covenant with God. (Read Mosiah 18:10.)
Application: We will write down the covenant of baptism that we have made and then read these additional scriptures on baptism: Matthew 3:11–17; Alma 6:2; 3 Nephi 7:24–26; 9:20; D&C 20:25; 33:11.

MONDAY

Purpose of the day: To understand that we must be worthy when we are baptized, or the covenant is void. (Read Moroni 6:1–3.)
Application: We will discuss baptism with our family and how each of us can prepare and make himself worthy of this ordinance. Hymn 236, "Lord, Accept into Thy Kingdom," can aid the discussion.

TUESDAY

Purpose of the day: To learn that when we are baptized, we are following Christ's example. (Read 2 Nephi 31:5, 9.)
Application: We will write a thank-you letter to our parents, the missionaries, the teacher, or any other person who helped set us a good example and helped us prepare for baptism.

WEDNESDAY

Purpose of the day: To learn that baptism must be by immersion. (Read 3 Nephi 11:26.)
Application: We will plan to attend the next baptismal service in our ward or branch.

THURSDAY

Purpose of the day: To learn that baptism symbolizes the death, burial, and resurrection of Christ. (Read D&C 76:51.)

Application: We will write down why we are happy to accept the responsibilities implied by baptism.

FRIDAY

Purpose of the day: To understand that we take Christ's name on ourselves when we are baptized. (Read 2 Nephi 31:13.)
Application: We will read 2 Nephi 31:19–20 to learn what taking Christ's name on ourselves means, and live up to this meaning in our lives.

SATURDAY

Purpose of the day: To learn that all men are to be baptized—following repentance—for a remission of sins. (Read D&C 49:13.)
Application: We will write a letter to a missionary from our ward or branch thanking him for teaching this commandment of the Lord.

For additional scriptures see Topical Guide, "Baptism."

Receiving the Holy Ghost
14

"The baptism of fire, without doubt, had reference to the purifying qualities of the Holy Ghost, which, like fire, consumes or destroys the unholy affections of those who are made partakers of it." (Orson Pratt, in Discourses on the Holy Ghost, Bookcraft, 1959, *p. 35.)*

DEFINITION
Receiving the Holy Ghost means having the Holy Ghost conferred upon us and receiving the right to its gifts as we are worthy.

WHY RECEIVE THE HOLY GHOST?
Without receiving the Holy ghost, we cannot enter into the celestial kingdom or the presence of the Lord. Baptism alone is not enough. In fact, unless we receive the Holy Ghost, we cannot even belong to the Church. Here again baptism alone is not enough. "God grants the gift of the Holy Ghost unto the obedient; and the bestowal of this gift follows faith, repentance, and baptism by water." (James E. Talmage, *Articles of Faith*, p. 163.)

PURPOSE OF THE WEEK

To understand what receiving the Holy Ghost means and to incorporate this understanding in our lives so that we might have the continual presence of the Holy Ghost.

SUNDAY

Purpose of the day: To learn that the Holy Ghost can be our constant companion. (Read D&C 121:46.)

Application: We will determine whether or not we have the constant companion of the Holy Ghost and then make a list of things to do that will help us to have this companionship. We will read these additional scriptures and ponder them in our hearts: Matthew 3:11; Acts 19:2–6; D&C 5:16.

MONDAY

Purpose of the day: To learn that when we receive the Holy Ghost we are following Christ's example. (Read Luke 3:21–22.)

Application: We will discuss with our family the gift of the Holy Ghost, especially in connection with following Christ's example. Hymn 236, "Lord, Accept into Thy Kingdom," can reinforce the discussion.

TUESDAY

Purpose of the day: To learn that the Holy Ghost is received following repentance and baptism. (Read D&C 19:31.)

Application: We will attend the next fast and testimony meeting in our ward or branch and listen carefully to the words used in confirming those who have been baptized. Then we will determine to repent of our own sins so that we might have the continued companionship of the Holy Ghost. (Read D&C 130:23.)

WEDNESDAY

Purpose of the day: To learn that the Holy Ghost is given through the laying on of hands by those with the authority to do so. (Read D&C 20:38, 41.)

Application: We will each trace back to Christ the authority of the person who confirmed us a member of the Church. We will also read Acts 8:17; D&C 35:6; Moroni 2:2–3.

THURSDAY

Purpose of the day: To learn that one does not receive the gift of the Holy Ghost before the age of eight, as this is the age of accountability set by the Lord. (Read D&C 68:27; Moroni 8:11.)

Application: We will write down reasons why we are accountable for our own actions and why those under eight years of age are not.

FRIDAY

Purpose of the day: To learn that the Holy Ghost is a personage of Spirit. (Read D&C 130:22.)

Application: We will thank the Lord in prayer for allowing the Holy Ghost to be in spirit form so that he might dwell with us and thus help and comfort us.

SATURDAY

Purpose of the day: To express appreciation for the gift of the Holy Ghost. (Read 2 Nephi 31:12.)

Application: We will promise the Lord that we will try to live worthy of his gift of the Holy Ghost.

For additional scriptures see Topical Guide, "Holy Ghost."

Born Again — True Conversion

15

"Man through the baptism of the water and of the Spirit is redeemed from ... spiritual death and by the power of the Holy Ghost, brought back into direct communion with God," and thus is born again. (Harold B. Lee, general conference, April 1961.)

DEFINITION
Born again in an ecclesiastical sense means a second birth or rebirth, born of God, becoming sons and daughters of Christ.

WHY BORN AGAIN?
The Inspired Version of the Bible states: "Whosoever is born of God doth not continue in sin; for the Spirit of God remaineth in him; and he cannot sin, because he is born of God, having received that holy Spirit of promise." (John 3:9.) Alma said that if we are "spiritually born of God," we will have God's image in our countenance and experience a "mighty change" in our hearts. (Alma 5:14.)

PURPOSE OF THE WEEK
To begin to become "born again—truly converted."

SUNDAY
Purpose of the day: To learn why we must be born again in order to inherit the kingdom of God. (Read John 3:5–7.)
Application: We will write down why being born again can be significant in our lives and will read these scriptures: Alma 7:14; Moses 6:59; Mosiah 5:7.

MONDAY
Purpose of the day: To learn that when we are born again, we make a change in our lives. (Read Ephesians 4:22–24.)
Application: We will discuss with our family how being born again means changing ourselves. Hymn 117, "Come Unto Jesus," can add to the discussion.

TUESDAY
Purpose of the day: To learn that being born again follows repentance. (Read Mosiah 27:24.)
Application: We will thank our Father in heaven for the opportunity to repent so that we might be reborn.

WEDNESDAY
Purpose of the day: To learn how we can truly know the Savior when we are born again. (Read D&C 93:1–2.)
Application: Each of us will write down our personal testimony of the Savior.

THURSDAY
Purpose of the day: To learn that being born again incorporates *true* conversion to the gospel. (Read 1 Peter 1:22–23.)
Application: We will determine whether or not we are truly converted to the gospel of Jesus Christ and then build for this great blessing. (See Moses 6:65.)

The Doctrine of Christ

FRIDAY

Purpose of the day: To learn that joy comes from true conversion and being born again. (Read Alma 36:24.)
Application: We will write down two or three blessings we can receive from being truly converted and born again.

SATURDAY

Purpose of the day: To learn that when we are converted, we must strengthen others. (Read Luke 22:31–32.)
Application: We will read and ponder these scriptures on converting others following our own conversion: Alma 5:49 and D&C 88:81.

For additional scriptures see Topical Guide, "Conversion."

How to Keep the Holy Ghost

16

To keep in tune with the Holy Ghost, we must keep the commandments.

DEFINITION
To keep the Holy Ghost means to preserve, maintain, and continue to hold his presence.

WHY KEEP THE HOLY GHOST?
The Holy Ghost "bears record of the Father and the Son, is our comfort in sorrow and distress, our strength in weakness, and our guide when in doubt." (Anthony W. Ivins, general conference address, October 1925.) Should we lose the Holy Ghost, we would lose the right to all the gifts of the Spirit, the right to receive inspiration and revelation from God, and the ability and/or right to gain eternal life and exaltation. If we strive to keep the Holy Ghost, then we will keep the right to all the gifts of the Spirit, the right to revelation and inspiration, and we will still retain the right and ability to gain eternal life and exaltation.

PURPOSE OF THE WEEK
To learn how to keep the Holy Ghost—to live by the Spirit.

SUNDAY
Purpose of the day: To gain a desire to keep the Holy Ghost. (Read 3 Nephi 19:9.)
Application: We will write down why we desire to have the Holy Ghost and will read these additional scriptures: Matthew 5:6; 2 Nephi 28:26; 3 Nephi 12:6; Alma 39:6; D&C 45:57–59; 132:27.

MONDAY
Purpose of the day: To learn that we must pray continually in order to keep the Holy Ghost. (Read D&C 63:64.)
Application: We will discuss with our family how prayer can help us keep the Holy Ghost. Hymn 98, "I Need Thee Every Hour," can add to the discussion.

TUESDAY
Purpose of the day: To learn that we must fast in order to keep the Holy Ghost. (Read Helaman 3:35.)
Application: We will fast in order to keep the Holy Ghost close to us.

WEDNESDAY
Purpose of the day: To learn that we must repent in order to keep the Holy Ghost. (Read D&C 1:33.)
Application: We will promise the Lord that we will repent so that we might continue to have the presence of the Holy Ghost to guide us in our daily lives.

THURSDAY
Purpose of the day: To learn that we must be obedient in order to keep the Holy Ghost. (Read Mosiah 5:5.)

Application: We will each write down two or three commandments we need to keep in order to be more diligent in obeying so that we might continue to have the presence of the Holy Ghost. (See D&C 130:21.)

FRIDAY

Purpose of the day: To learn how remembering the Savior helps us to keep the Holy Ghost. (Read 3 Nephi 18:11.)
Application: We will write down why remembering the Savior will help us keep the presence of the Holy Ghost.

SATURDAY

Purpose of the day: To learn that denying the Holy Ghost is unforgivable. (Read Matthew 12:31–32.)
Application: We will promise the Lord that we will do all we can to keep the Holy Ghost and live righteously so that we might never have the terrible experience of committing the "unpardonable sin." (See also Hebrews 6:4–6.)

For additional scriptures see Topical Guide, "Holy Ghost"; "Holy Spirit."

Revelation

17

"We believe all that God has revealed, all that He does now reveal, and we believe that He will yet reveal many great and important things pertaining to the Kingdom of God." (Article of Faith 9.)

DEFINITION
"... revelation signifies the making known of divine truth by communication from the heavens." (James E. Talmage, *Articles of Faith*, p. 296.)

WHY REVELATION?
Without revelation, how can man learn of God and know his current will or what he wants done on the earth? "Behold, great and marvelous are the works of the Lord. How unsearchable are the depths of the mysteries of him; and it is impossible that man should find out all his ways. And no man knoweth of his ways save it be revealed unto him; wherefore, brethren, despise not the revelations of God." (Jacob 4:8.) The Lord reveals to the prophets how he wants his church run, what his commandments are, and what he wants people to

do. To each person who asks faithfully he also reveals what he wants that person to do with and in his life, with his own problems and in his sphere of influence (home, work, classroom, Church assignment, etc.). It is through revelation (which can come as inspiration, visions, dreams, by voice, etc.) that the Lord tells people what he wants. This is greater than all knowledge of man; therefore, let us receive the revelations of God.

PURPOSE OF THE WEEK

To understand revelation and how it can affect us in our daily lives.

SUNDAY

Purpose of the day: To learn that man needs revelation in order to know God. (Read 1 Corinthians 1:20–21.)
Application: Those with worldly wisdom do not know God or even *of* him. When someone wants to know of God and to know God himself, he gains this knowledge through revelation. We will ask the Lord, through faith, if he will confirm our testimony of his existence. (See Moroni 10:5; Isaiah 55:6; Joel 2:28–29; John 16:13; 1 Nephi 15:3, 7–11; 2 Nephi 9:28–29; D&C 50:23–24.)

MONDAY

Purpose of the day: To learn how revelation is needed to know the *will* of God. (Read 1 Corinthians 2:10–13.)
Application: We will discuss with our family why revelation is necessary to know God and to know his will. Hymns 271, "Oh, Holy Words of Truth and Love," and 21, "Come Listen to a Prophet's Voice," can reinforce the discussion.

TUESDAY

Purpose of the day: To learn how God reveals his word through his prophets. (Read Amos 3:7.)

Application: We will discuss how the president of the Church is a prophet of the Lord who receives revelation from the Lord, and the importance of following his counsel.

WEDNESDAY

Purpose of the day: To understand that we can receive personal revelation for ourselves. (Read D&C 42:61; 8:1–3.)

Application: We will record in our journals at least one time when we have received personal revelation from the heavens (an answer to a prayer, direction on something we should do).

THURSDAY

Purpose of the day: To learn that we may obtain a revelation from the Lord only after we desire and seek it. (Read 1 Nephi 10:17, 19; 11:1.)

Application: Seek earnestly, through study and with prayer and fasting, to know the will of God, and he *will* answer us.

FRIDAY

Purpose of the day: To learn that we must be prepared to receive revelation. (Read Alma 5:46.)

Application: We cannot just receive revelation whenever we want it unless we are prepared to receive it. In addition to preparing ourselves to receive the revelation, we must learn to listen for the answer he will give. As one man put it, sometimes our minds are so crowded with our own thoughts that God's cannot get through. We will write down what we need to do to prepare to receive personal revelation from the Lord. (See Matthew 13:10–15; 2 Nephi 33:2.)

SATURDAY

Purpose of the day: To be willing to accept the revelations of God. (Read D&C 132:3.)

Application: We will promise the Lord that we will accept and obey his revelations and instructions. (See D&C 82:4; Jacob 4:10; Alma 37:37.)

For additional scriptures see Topical Guide, "Revelation."

God's Plan for Man

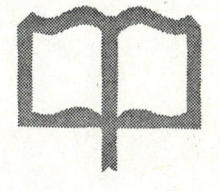

God Is All Powerful

18

"For, unless God had power over all things, and was able, by his power, to control all things, . . . men could not be saved. . . . " (Joseph Smith, Lecture on Faith 4.)

DEFINITION
To be all-powerful means to have total knowledge, wisdom, and control in regard to man's existence, through obedience to all laws.

WHY GOD IS ALL-POWERFUL
Joseph Smith stated that if God were not all-powerful, he would not have been able to create the worlds that are, have been, and will be, nor could he have put forth the plan of salvation and made it effective. Men must put their faith and trust in God, "believing that he has power to save all who come to him, to the very uttermost." (Lecture on Faith, no 4.) Those who do not believe in God's power never really looked at the earth around them, at the universe above, or really took a good look at man himself. "And now behold, can ye dispute

the power of God?... and they knew that there was nothing save the power of God that could shake the earth and cause it to tremble as though it would part asunder." (Mosiah 27:15, 18.) "The earth is the Lord's, and the fulness thereof; the world, and they that dwell therein." (Psalm 24:1.) God uses his power to help us because he loves us and wants us to return to him.

PURPOSE OF THE WEEK
To learn what blessings come from God's being all-powerful.

SUNDAY
Purpose of the day: To learn that God is all-powerful. (Read Moses 1:3; Isaiah 14:24, 27.)
Application: We will write down why it is important to us that God is all-powerful and will then read these scriptures about God: 1 Chronicles 29:11–12; Romans 1:20; Enos 1:23, 26; D&C 50:27.

MONDAY
Purpose of the day: To learn that because God is all-powerful, he is unchanging. (Read Malachi 3:6.)
Application: Joseph Smith stated that God "changes not, neither is there variableness with him; but that he is the same from everlasting to everlasting, being the same yesterday, to-day and forever; and that his course is one eternal round, without variation." (Lecture on Faith, no. 3.) We will discuss with our family this statement from the Prophet and how God is unchanging in knowledge, power, goodness, his relationship to man, mercy, and fairness. Hymn 68, "A Mighty Fortress Is Our God," can reinforce the discussion.

TUESDAY
Purpose of the day: To learn that because God is all-powerful, he is perfect. (Read 3 Nephi 12:48.)
Application: We will make a list of several things we need to accomplish to become more perfect and will begin to work on these one at a time.

WEDNESDAY

Purpose of the day: To learn that God is all-powerful and all-knowing. (Read Romans 11:33.)

Application: We will each set a goal and schedule for studying the scriptures and/or some other good books in order to gain knowledge and increase our intelligence and will begin to follow the schedule. We will read Abraham 3:19; Moses 1:6; Acts 15:18; Romans 11:33–36; 2 Nephi 9:20.

THURSDAY

Purpose of the day: To learn that because God is all-powerful, he has all the characteristics associated with goodness and greatness. (Read D&C 84:102.)

Application: We will make a list of all the attributes of God we would like to achieve and will then begin working toward attaining these characteristics.

FRIDAY

Purpose of the day: To learn that all things were created by the power of God. (Read Moses 1:30–33.)

Application: We will read Moses 1 and D&C 88:45–47 and decide what these passages mean to us in our lives.

SATURDAY

Purpose of the day: To learn that denial of the power of God brings punishment. (Read Jacob 6:8–10.)

Application: We will write down some of the things happening around the world today that indicate that people are denying the power of God and thus are going to merit his eternal punishment.

For additional scriptures see Topical Guide, "God, Power of"; "Power."

God of Love, Mercy, and Justice

19

One of the greatest motives for a righteous life is the knowledge of God and his attributes as he relates to his children.

DEFINITION

God's love is his benevolent and tender affection for his children. His mercy means his forbearance from inflicting harm and his compassionate treatment of his children, including forgiveness and clemency. His justice means his equitable reward or punishment for obedience or disobedience to his rules, laws, and commandments.

WHY A GOD OF LOVE, MERCY, AND JUSTICE?

God gave the children of men a plan of salvation because he loves them. He wants them to become as he is. Justice and mercy are a part of that plan, which includes his laws and commandments. "And if there was no law given, if men sinned what could justice do, or mercy either, for they would have no claim upon the creature? But there is a law given, and a punishment affixed, and a repentance granted; which repentance mercy claimeth; otherwise, justice claimeth the creature and executeth the law, and the law inflicteth the punishment; if not so, the works of justice would be destroyed, and God would cease to be God." (Alma 42:21–22.) In other words, the scriptures say that because God loves his children, he gives laws and commandments for them to obey; and if they obey these laws and commandments, they receive their reward. If they disobey, they are punished because of the justice of God. However, if they repent of their disobedience, then the mercy of God intervenes and they are not punished. This whole balance is achieved through the atonement of Christ and was given to man because of God's love. "There is no fear in love; but perfect love casteth out fear:... We love [God], because he first loved us." (1 John 4:18–19.)

PURPOSE OF THE WEEK

To learn how God's love, mercy, and justice can affect our lives.

SUNDAY

Purpose of the day: To learn that God is characterized by love: he loves his children. (Read 1 Nephi 11:22, 1 John 4:16.)
Application: We will write down our testimonies of the love of God and then read John 3:16; 1 John 4:7–21; Ephesians 2:4; Jacob 3:2; D&C 6:20.

MONDAY

Purpose of the day: To learn that God is motivated by love in all that he does. (Read 2 Nephi 26:24; D&C 95:1; Proverbs 3:11–12; Hebrews 12:6.)
Application: We will discuss with our family the love of God and how it is reflected in what he does. Verse 3 of hymn 20, "God of Power, God of Right," can contribute to the discussion.

TUESDAY

Purpose of the day: To learn how repentance brings the mercy of God. (Read Ether 11:8; D&C 61:2.)
Application: We will resolve in writing to repent so that we may obtain the mercy of the Lord.

WEDNESDAY

Purpose of the day: To give thanks to God for his mercy. (Read Psalm 106:1.)
Application: We will give thanks to God with all our heart for his mercy to us and to all mankind.

THURSDAY

Purpose of the day: To learn that no one is exempt from the justice of God. (Read D&C 107:84.)
Application: Justice is the reward or punishment meted out for obedience or disobedience to the laws and commandments of God. We will write down why we are glad that God is just and dispenses his justice equitably.

FRIDAY

Purpose of the day: To learn that the justice of God divides the righteous from the wicked. (Read Alma 41:2.)
Application: We will resolve to live righteously so that when the judgment comes, we will be on the Lord's side and not separated from his presence.

SATURDAY

Purpose of the day: To learn that the justice of God requires men to be judged for their own works and actions. (Read Alma 41:3–4.)
Application: We will write down those actions we wish to change or improve upon so that we might merit happiness and joy at the judgment day.

For additional scriptures see Topical Guide, "God, Love of"; "God, Mercy of."

The Fall
20

"... Christ came to ransom men from the temporal and spiritual death brought into the world by the fall of Adam...." (Joseph Fielding Smith, general conference address, April 1971.)

DEFINITION
The transgression of Adam brought about the mortal state of man.

WHY THE FALL?
The Fall was a part of the Lord's plan decided upon before the world began. Men had to learn to make choices, and this came through the Fall. Without the Fall, there would have been no people on the earth. Without the Fall, there would have been no transgression, no death, no Savior, no plan of salvation, no resurrection, and no exaltation. In fact, without the Fall, God's plans would have come to naught. And because man is in a fallen state, he must repent and return to God, or he will remain in that fallen state forever.

PURPOSE OF THE WEEK

To learn what the Fall means in our lives and how we can overcome our fallen state.

SUNDAY

Purpose of the day: To learn that mankind exists because of the Fall. (Read 2 Nephi 2:25.)
Application: We will thank our Father in heaven for our existence on the earth today and will read Moses 6:48; 5:11; 1 Timothy 2:14–15.

MONDAY

Purpose of the day: To learn that the Fall came because of Adam's transgression. (Read D&C 29:40.)
Application: We will discuss with our family how the Fall came about and then discuss with them the second Article of Faith. Hymn 68, "A Mighty Fortress Is Our God," can be of help in the discussion.

TUESDAY

Purpose of the day: To learn that all mankind is in a fallen state. (Read 1 Nephi 10:6.)
Application: We will discuss and write down why Christ was the only person who has lived on the earth who did not sin.

WEDNESDAY

Purpose of the day: To learn that disobedience keeps man in a fallen state. (Read Alma 42:12.)
Application: We will list the causes of our disobedience and then make a plan to overcome these weaknesses.

THURSDAY

Purpose of the day: To learn that a fallen state means a person is carnal, sensual, and devilish. (Read D&C 20:20.)

Application: We will write down how a person changes from a fallen state to a righteous one. (Read Mosiah 27:25.)

FRIDAY

Purpose of the day: To learn that life is a probationary period to see if we can overcome our fallen state. (Read Alma 12:24; Moses 6:50.)

Application: We will write down one thing of which we need to repent, and then do so.

SATURDAY

Purpose of the day: To learn that the Messiah came to redeem mankind from the fall. (Read 2 Nephi 2:6.)

Application: We will thank our Father in heaven in prayer for Christ's redemption of mankind.

For additional scriptures see Topical Guide, "Fall"; "Fall of Man."

Temptations

21

"When temptations come to you, be humble and faithful and determined that you will overcome, and you will receive a deliverance and continue faithful, having the promise of receiving blessings." (Brigham Young, Journal of Discourses, *16:164.)*

DEFINITION

Temptation means to be persuaded, enticed, or induced into evil or sin; it includes being led or provoked into doing something wrong.

WHY TEMPTATIONS?

Life is a probationary state in which man must overcome evil. (See Alma 42:10.) The Lord has said, "And we will prove [mankind] herewith, to see if they will do all things whatsoever the Lord their God shall command them." (Abraham 3:25.) In other words, man must be able to make a choice and follow either God or Satan. Each person has choices to make, often several times a day, in big and little things.

PURPOSE OF THE WEEK
To help us learn to overcome temptations.

SUNDAY
Purpose of the day: To learn that temptations are necessary for the free agency of man. (Read D&C 29:39; 2 Nephi 2: 11, 16.)
Application: We will read James 1:12–15, especially verse 13, about temptation being not of God, and will then read these other scriptures: Moses 4:4; D&C 10:22–27.

MONDAY
Purpose of the day: To learn though Christ was tempted, he did not fall. (Read D&C 20:22.)
Application: We will discuss with our family how we can follow Christ's example in resisting temptation. Hymns 97, "Lead, Kindly Light," and 98, "I Need Thee Every Hour," can assist with this concept.

TUESDAY
Purpose of the day: To learn that Satan uses various enticements to tempt people to do wrong. (Read 3 Nephi 3:15–16.)
Application: Some of the enticements Satan uses to tempt people include power, authority, riches (1 Timothy 6:9), pride (D&C 23:1), and fear of persecution by neighbors and the world (D&C 40:2). He will use any one or combinations of these things to tempt people into sin. We will each write down two weaknesses we have and will then strive to overcome these weaknesses and become stronger persons so that we won't fall into temptation.

WEDNESDAY
Purpose of the day: We must watch and pray always to resist temptation. (Read Mark 14:38.)
Application: The Lord has repeatedly said in the scriptures to watch and pray, lest we be led into temptation. He said to pray

daily (Alma 31:10) and continuously (Alma 13:28) in order to resist temptation. The Lord's Prayer says, "And lead us not into temptation, but deliver us from evil...." (Matthew 6:13.) We will pray this night and always that we will be able to resist temptations and keep on the path of righteousness.

THURSDAY

Purpose of the day: To learn how righteous living will help us resist temptations. (Read 1 Nephi 15:24.)
Application: Christ said when we break the commandment of coming unto him, we can be led into temptation (3 Nephi 18:25); and the prophets said that if we are wise in the days of our probation, we will serve the Lord and not yield to temptation (Mormon 9:28). We will commit ourselves to live more righteous lives so that we may resist the temptations that come our way.

FRIDAY

Purpose of the day: To learn how we may not be tempted above what we are able to bear *if* we are striving to serve the Lord. (Read 1 Corinthians 10:13.)
Application: We will thank the Lord for helping us resist at least one temptation we were faced with this particular day.

SATURDAY

Purpose of the day: To learn that we can withstand temptation by holding to the rod. (Read Alma 37:33; 1 Nephi 8:23; 2 Nephi 32:3.)
Application: Through study, we will get closer to the Lord. We will thus evaluate our study time and resolve to make more effective use of it.

For additional scriptures see Topical Guide, "Tempt"; "Temptation."

The Plan of Salvation

22

"For as in Adam all die, even so in Christ shall all be made alive." (1 Corinthians 15:22.) "This gospel is the plan of salvation. It was ordained and established in the councils of eternity before the foundations of this earth were laid, and it has been revealed anew in our day for the salvation and blessing of our Father's children everywhere." (Joseph Fielding Smith, general conference address, October 1971.)

DEFINITION
Salvation is when a man is saved from spiritual consequences of his sins through repentance. It includes deliverance from the second or eternal death through the atonement of Christ; in other words, redemption, progression, and resurrection.

WHY THE PLAN OF SALVATION?
If we follow the plan of salvation, we may gain eternal life and exaltation and live again with our Father in heaven. If we reject

or do not follow this plan given by the Lord, we will gain a lesser degree of glory, or possibly not even gain one at all. It is a fact that "God would cease to be God if he could sweep aside a man's record who is unrepentant and extend to him salvation or exaltation. He would violate the eternal law. He is bound by law, and he can only come to the aid and help of men and women who have conformed to the eternal law by which these same blessings and privileges may be extended." (Melvin J. Ballard, *Sermons and Missionary Services*, p. 221.) For, as the scriptures say, "There is a law, irrevocably decreed in heaven before the foundations of this world, upon which all blessings are predicated—And when we obtain any blessing from God, it is by obedience to that law upon which it is predicated." (D&C 130:20-21.)

PURPOSE OF THE WEEK

To learn of the plan of salvation given for the benefit of mankind, and to be grateful and take advantage of it.

SUNDAY

Purpose of the day: To learn that the plan of salvation is the main purpose for God's existence. (Read Moses 1:39; Alma 24:14.)

Application: We will vow that we will love the Lord and keep his commandments because he loves us and has given us the plan of salvation. These scriptures will help us understand this important principle: Psalm 37:39; Romans 1:16; 2 Nephi 4:30; Alma 9:28; D&C 20:29; 82:9.

MONDAY

Purpose of the day: To learn that God is the author of the plan of salvation. (Read Alma 12:30.)

Application: With our family, we will discuss the plan of salvation, God's authorship of it, and Christ's implementation of it. Hymns 78, "God of Our Fathers, Whose Almighty Hand,"

and 258, "O Thou Rock of Our Salvation," can help reinforce the concept.

TUESDAY

Purpose of the day: To learn that the plan of salvation is centered in Christ. (Read Moses 6:62.)
Application: We will write down why we think that Christ is the center of the plan of salvation.

WEDNESDAY

Purpose of the day: To learn that the priesthood holds the keys to the plan of salvation. (Read D&C 128:11.)
Application: The priesthood is the power of God on earth, and its purpose is to bless people's lives. The plan includes the fall of Adam and the atonement of Christ (1 Corinthians 15:22; Moses 6:59), repentance, faith, baptism, the gift of the Holy Ghost, worshipping God in the name of Christ, enduring to the end (D&C 20:29; 2 Nephi 9:23–24; Moses 6:59–62), and eternal marriage (D&C 131:1–4). We will write down how the priesthood has blessed each of us in our lives.

THURSDAY

Purpose of the day: To learn that personal effort is needed in order to follow the plan of salvation. (Read D&C 123:17.)
Application: We will make a commitment to the Lord that we will try to follow his plan and thus be able to return to his presence.

FRIDAY

Purpose of the day: To learn that the plan of salvation is to be taught to the world. (Read Mosiah 15:28.)
Application: We will attempt to live for one day as a perfect example of the precepts of the plan of salvation, and will write a letter to a nonmember friend.

SATURDAY

Purpose of the day: To learn that the plan of salvation is revealed through the scriptures and the words of the prophets. (Read D&C 35:20; Jarom 2.)

Application: We will memorize one scripture about the plan of salvation.

For additional scriptures see Topical Guide, "Gospel"; "Plan"; "Salvation, Plan of."

Jesus Christ, Our Savior

23

"... salvation is in Christ, It comes because of the infinite and eternal atonement which he wrought by the shedding of his blood. He is the Son of God, and he came into the world to ransom men from the temporal and spiritual death that came because of what we call the fall." (Joseph Fielding Smith, general conference address, October 1971.)

DEFINITION
The Savior is "that Christ who came to ransom men from ... temporal and spiritual death...." (Ibid.)

WHY JESUS CHRIST, OUR SAVIOR?
"Jesus, the Christ: In the beginning with God; himself God; author of our salvation and exaltation; creator of the world and all that in it is; the light and life of the world; our Savior, dying on the cross for us, our intercessor with the Father, who time and again said: 'This is my beloved Son, hear him'; bestower of infinite love and mercy; soul of compassion and forgiveness; healer of sick bodies and broken hearts; friend

of the friendless; giver of divine peace, his peace. God grant to each of us this knowledge, this testimony." (J. Reuben Clark, Jr., *Behold the Lamb of God,* Deseret Book, 1962, preface.)

PURPOSE OF THE WEEK
To know Jesus Christ, our Savior, so that we might emulate him.

SUNDAY
Purpose of the day: To learn that Christ was the Firstborn in the spirit world and was foreordained for his mission on earth. (Read D&C 93:21; 1 Peter 1:17–20.)
Application: We will write down our feelings about Christ as our Elder Brother. We will also read these scriptures about Christ: Isaiah 45:20–25; Hebrews 1:2–3; Mosiah 3:5–12; Moses 1:6.

MONDAY
Purpose of the day: To learn that Christ was the Creator of this and other worlds under the direction of the Father. (Read Mosiah 4:2.)
Application: We will discuss with our family the creation of the earth by the Savior under God's direction, as one aspect of his being the Savior of mankind. We will also read Moses 1:32–33. Hymns 101, "Jesus, My Savior True," and 181, "Jesus of Nazareth, Savior and King," can be of benefit in the discussion.

TUESDAY
Purpose of the day: To learn that Jesus is our advocate with the Father. (Read D&C 45:3–5.)
Application: We will look up in a dictionary what the word *advocate* means and find all the synonyms we can.

WEDNESDAY
Purpose of the day: To learn that Christ is the God of this earth. (Read 3 Nephi 11:14; Moses 1.)

Application: We will read Isaiah 45:15; 3 Nephi 15:4–5; 1 Nephi 13:41; Alma 5:50; and 3 Nephi 22:5, which tell about Christ's being the God of this earth, and will then decide why this is important to us.

THURSDAY

Purpose of the day: To learn that Christ is the Only Begotten of the Father in the flesh. (Read John 1:14.)

Application: Even though all the people on the earth are spirit children of the Father, Christ is the only one who is literally the physical Son of God. He had immortal characteristics from his Father and mortal ones from his mother. Therefore, because he had powers both from on high and on earth, he was able to give his life and to take it up again for mankind. We will list why it is important that Christ is the Only Begotten in the flesh.

FRIDAY

Purpose of the day: To learn that Christ is the Messiah, the Lamb of God. (Read 1 Nephi 12:18.)

Application: We will write down how we know that Christ is the Lamb of God, the Messiah, and what this means in our lives.

SATURDAY

Purpose of the day: To learn and understand that Jesus Christ is the Savior of mankind. (Read 1 John 4:14; D&C 43:34; Moses 1:39.)

Application: We will read Acts 4:12; Mosiah 3:17; and D&C 18:21–23; then we will ponder these scriptures and thank our Father in heaven for sending Jesus Christ that mankind may take his name upon themselves and be saved.

For additional scriptures see Topical Guide, "Jesus Christ, Redeemer."

"Come, Follow Me"
24

Jesus Christ was the Master Teacher, the great example, the Savior of mankind. We should follow his example in all things and, through his priesthood, do all things necessary to build his kingdom.

DEFINITION
An example is something that is followed and/or imitated, a pattern or model set up to guide us.

WHY FOLLOW CHRIST AND HIS EXAMPLE?
Christ set the example and told us to follow him. "And he said unto the children of men: Follow thou me. Wherefore, my beloved brethren, can we follow Jesus save we shall be willing to keep the commandments of the Father?" (2 Nephi 31:10.) If we cannot follow Christ, how can we expect to enter the celestial kingdom, for he is the one who shows the way, who directs the path, and who guides those who enter therein. (See Matthew 7:14.) Only those who follow Christ will be able to find exaltation with the Father. How may we follow Christ? By keeping his commandments, as the scriptures state.

God's Plan for Man

PURPOSE OF THE WEEK
To learn to follow Christ and to do as he would do.

SUNDAY
Purpose of the day: To learn that Christ set the example; he is the Great Exemplar. (Read 3 Nephi 18:16.)
Application: We will read these scriptures about following Christ's example: D&C 124:53–54; 2 Nephi 31:10, 16; 3 Nephi 27:27; Mormon 7:10; 1 Peter 2:21–25; John 13:15. Then we will write down how each one of these scriptures can be applied in our lives today.

MONDAY
Purpose of the day: To learn that Jesus Christ is the Master Teacher. (Read John 3:2.)
Application: We will discuss with our family the role of Christ as the Master Teacher and Great Exemplar, and how the whole family can follow him. Hymn 116, "Come, Follow Me," will aid the discussion.

TUESDAY
Purpose of the day: To learn how Jesus is a friend to the friendless. (Read Matthew 9:10–13.)
Application: We will make it a point to be especially friendly to everyone for one whole day.

WEDNESDAY
Purpose of the day: To learn that Christ is the great healer. (Read 3 Nephi 17:7–9.)
Application: For the rest of this week, we will follow the example of Christ and be cheerful and happy, helping and healing, rather than destructive, in all our actions.

THURSDAY
Purpose of the day: To learn that Jesus Christ is the giver of peace, the Prince of Peace. (Read John 14:27.)

Application: Christ said, "Blessed are the peacemakers: for they shall be called the children of God." (Matthew 5:9.) He was the Prince of Peace. (Isaiah 9:6.) We will ponder this concept and how it can give us peace on earth and in heaven.

FRIDAY

Purpose of the day: To learn and understand that Jesus Christ is full of love for all mankind. (Read John 15:9–10.)
Application: We will read Matthew 5:43–44; 19:19; 22:37–40; and 1 John 4:20–21. Then we will write down scriptures on love in our daily lives and thus show love, in order that we might receive the love of Christ.

SATURDAY

Purpose of the day: To learn that Jesus Christ is the light of the world. (Read D&C 11:28.)
Application: We will write down why Jesus Christ is the light of the world and how, specifically, we can let our own lights shine to bless others.

For additional scriptures see Topical Guide, "Jesus Christ, Teaching Mode of"; "Jesus Christ, Relationships with the Father"; "Jesus Christ, Atonement through"; "Jesus Christ, Good Shepherd"; "Jesus Christ, Exemplar."

Atonement

25

"A man, as a man, could arrive at all the dignity that a man was capable of obtaining or receiving; but it needed a God to raise him to the dignity of a God." (John Taylor, The Mediation and Atonement of Christ, *Stevens and Wallis, 1950, p. 143.)*

DEFINITION
Atonement is the redeeming effect of Christ's suffering, death, and resurrection, and includes Christ's mediation between God and man.

WHY ATONEMENT?
The atonement is the mainstay of the gospel; in fact, according to the scriptures, it is the gospel itself. "And this is the gospel, the glad tidings, which the voice out of the heavens bore record unto us—That he came into the world, even Jesus, to be crucified for the world, and to bear the sins of the world, and to sanctify the world, and to cleanse it from all unrighteousness; That through him all might be saved whom the Father had put into his power and made by him." (D&C 76:40–42.) In

fact, without the atonement, "all mankind must be lost." (Jacob 7:12.) Therefore, in order for mankind to be saved from both spiritual and temporal death and to return again to the Father, the atonement was made by Jesus Christ.

PURPOSE OF THE WEEK

To learn of the atonement and our responsibility toward it.

SUNDAY

Purpose of the day: To learn that the atonement was necessary because of the fall of Adam. (Read 2 Nephi 2:25–26; Alma 42:9.)
Application: We will write down why the atonement was necessary for our own salvation from the fall of Adam, and will read these scriptures on the atonement: Moses 5:9; 6:54; D&C 29:40–42.

MONDAY

Purpose of the day: To learn that Christ suffered for the sins of the world. (Read Isaiah 53:4–6; 1 John 2:2.)
Application: With our family we will discuss the atonement and what Christ suffered for us. Hymn 196, "Jesus, Once of Humble Birth," helps tell the story.

TUESDAY

Purpose of the day: To learn that Christ had power over death. (Read John 10:17–18.)
Application: Why was it necessary for Christ to have power over death in order for the atonement to be effective? We will write down why we appreciate Christ's power over death and how it applies to us.

WEDNESDAY

Purpose of the day: To learn that the atonement was motivated by God's love for his children. (Read John 3:16–17.)
Application: We will each do something special for someone we love. We will also read John 15:13; 1 John 3:16; and D&C

34:3, which tell how Christ loved the world and its inhabitants and laid down his life for them.

THURSDAY

Purpose of the day: To learn that all men benefit from the atonement. (Read Moses 5:9.)

Application: Everyone who has lived on this earth, who is now living, or who will yet live on the earth will be resurrected and will be saved from the temporal death caused by the fall of Adam. We will write down the difference between temporal and spiritual death. (Read Alma 42:9 and Alma 11:42.)

FRIDAY

Purpose of the day: To learn that men must repent in order to take full benefit from the atonement. (Read D&C 19:15–20.)

Application: We will make a vow to repent of our sins from this time forth.

SATURDAY

Purpose of the day: To learn that if we knowingly reject the atonement, we must suffer, even as Christ did. (Read D&C 19:17.)

Application: We will promise God that we will never knowingly reject the atonement of Christ. (Read Alma 11:41 and Mosiah 15:26.)

For additional scriptures see Topical Guide, "Atonement"; "Jesus Christ, Atonement through."

Sacrament

26

"The partaking of the sacrament of the Lord's Supper is one of the most sacred ordinances of the Church of Christ," (David O. McKay, Millennial Star, *December 6, 1923, p. 776.)*

DEFINITION
The sacrament is a sacred ordinance. The bread and water are emblems that represent the Lord's body and blood and are partaken of in remembrance of him.

WHY SACRAMENT?
In partaking of the sacrament, we recovenant to Jesus Christ by remembering him and promising to keep his commandments, thus drawing closer to him. It is an ordinance vital to our eternal life.

PURPOSE OF THE WEEK
To learn what the sacrament means and to put this meaning into action in our lives.

SUNDAY

Purpose of the day: To partake of the sacrament on the Lord's day. (Read D&C 20:75.)
Application: We will each make it a point to think exclusively about Christ when we take the sacrament. (Read D&C 59:9; Mosiah 18:7–10; 1 Corinthians 11:27–30.)

MONDAY

Purpose of the day: To learn that Christ instituted the sacrament, or Lord's Supper. (Read 1 Corinthians 11:23–25.)
Application: We will discuss with our family the sacrament and what it means, and will sing our favorite sacrament hymn to accentuate the meaning of the discussion.

TUESDAY

Purpose of the day: To learn that the bread and water of the sacrament are emblems of Christ's flesh and blood. (Read D&C 20:40.)
Application: We will list reasons why the representation of the bread and water for the flesh and blood of Christ is important to us.

WEDNESDAY

Purpose of the day: To learn about the covenants we make with the Lord when we partake of the sacrament. (Read D&C 20:77; Moroni 4:3.)
Application: The covenants we make when we partake of the sacrament include these three: (1) to remember Christ's broken body and the blood that he shed, (2) to take Christ's name upon ourselves, and (3) to keep God's commandments. We will write down which (if any) of these three covenants we have broken during the last week and will resolve to keep all three from now on.

THURSDAY

Purpose of the day: To learn of the promises the Lord makes to those who keep the covenants made when partaking of the sacrament. (Read D&C 20:79; Moroni 5:2.)

Application: When we partake worthily of the sacrament, the Lord promises that (1) his Spirit will be with us and (2) we shall have eternal life. We will promise the Lord that we will partake of the sacrament worthily, so that we might enjoy these blessings.

FRIDAY

Purpose of the day: To learn why we must not partake of the sacrament unworthily. (Read 3 Nephi 18:28–29.)

Application: The prophets and Christ have said that when we partake of the sacrament unworthily, we are personally taking Christ's life. We cannot partake worthily if we have not made reconciliation for transgressions committed. (See D&C 46:4.) We will make prompt restitution for any transgressions we have committed this week so we will be able to partake worthily of the sacrament on Sunday.

SATURDAY

Purpose of the day: To learn that taking the sacrament can help us gain eternal life. (Read John 6:54; D&C 27:2.)

Application: We will write down why partaking of the sacrament worthily is a step toward eternal life.

For additional scriptures see Topical Guide, "Sacrament."

Resurrection and Judgment

27

"And it is requisite with the justice of God that men should be judged according to their works; and if their works were good in this life, and the desires of their hearts were good, that they should also, at the last day, be restored unto that which is good." (Alma 41:3.)

DEFINITION
Resurrection means being raised from the dead to immortality. Christ was the first to rise.

WHY RESURRECTION AND JUDGMENT?
Without the resurrection, men would not be able to return to live with their Father in heaven. God will judge each person to see which degree of glory he or she will attain, dependent on their life on the earth, their works, their behavior, and their beliefs. The *resurrection* is the beginning of the immortal soul. Not all men will be resurrected at the same time, "but every

man in his own order" (1 Corinthians 15:23), and each will be judged and will attain that glory which he has earned. The resurrection will be the gift from Christ for those who kept their first estate, and exaltation will come to those who obey God's laws and commandments here on the earth.

PURPOSE OF THE WEEK

To learn about the resurrection and the judgment, in order that we might work toward eternal life and gain blessings instead of condemnation at the judgment seat.

SUNDAY

Purpose of the day: To learn that the resurrection was brought about by Christ. (Read Mosiah 15:20.)

Application: The resurrection, which was part of the plan of salvation formulated before the world began, could only be brought about by Christ because he had an immortal Father and a mortal mother. Read the following scriptures that explain this concept: 2 Nephi 9:5–7; Jacob 4:11–12; D&C 76:39; D&C 88:96–98; 1 Corinthians 15:12–23.

MONDAY

Purpose of the day: To learn that the resurrection is an unconditional gift from Christ to all mankind. (Read 2 Nephi 9:22.)

Application: We will discuss with our family the resurrection, especially as being a gift given by Christ. Hymns 200, "Christ the Lord Is Risen Today," and 199, "He is Risen," can help reinforce the discussion.

TUESDAY

Purpose of the day: To learn that the resurrection is a reuniting of the spirit and the body. (Read Alma 11:43, 45.)

Application: We will discuss why it is important to us that the resurrection is a reuniting of the body and spirit. (Read Ezekiel 37:5–6.)

WEDNESDAY

Purpose of the day: To learn that there is a space between death and resurrection. (Read Alma 40:6.)

Application: What did Christ mean when he told the thief on the cross, "Verily I say unto thee, To day shalt thou be with me in paradise" (Luke 23:43)? He spoke about that place of rest which comes between death and the resurrection, that season when those who lived righteous lives on the earth would have a time and a place to rest, and when those who had not lived righteous lives will have a chance to hear the missionaries and try to repent (even though repentance is much harder in the spirit than in the body). We will promise God that we will live the kind of life that will enable us to rest in paradise.

THURSDAY

Purpose of the day: To learn that each person should gain knowledge about the resurrection and the world to come. (Read Jacob 4:12.)

Application: We will write down three things we need to do to prepare to face God at the judgment and then begin doing those three things.

FRIDAY

Purpose of the day: To learn that all people must stand before the judgment bar of God. (Read 3 Nephi 26:4.)

Application: We will continue preparing ourselves to meet God by doing the things we have already listed (a continuation of Thursday's application).

SATURDAY

Purpose of the day: To learn that each person will be judged for his own works, whatever they might be, and not for someone else's. (Read Mosiah 16:10.)

Application: We will write down that judgment which we wish: happiness and blessings or punishment and despair. We will then continue working to achieve our goal.

For additional scriptures see Topical Guide, "Resurrection"; "Judgment."

Our Ultimate Goal: Exaltation

28

Eternal life is God's life, the power to beget spirit children, the power to create worlds, as God the Father and his Son Jesus Christ created this world.

DEFINITION
The degrees of glory are those places of reward inherited or merited by a person's actions and works upon the earth. Exaltation means being raised or elevated to a higher state, place, power, and glory.

WHY EXALTATION?
"The ultimatum of our travel in this path of exaltation will bring to us the fullness of our Lord Jesus Christ, to stand in the presence of our Father, to receive of His fullness, to have the pleasure of increasing in our posterity worlds without end, to enjoy those pleasant associations that we have had in this life, to have our sons and daughters, our husbands and wives, surrounded with all the enjoyment that heaven can bestow,

our bodies glorified like unto the Savior's, free from disease and all the ills of life, and free from the disappointments and vexations and the unpleasant sacrifices that we are making here." (Lorenzo Snow, *Millennial Star,* August 24, 1899 [vol. 61], p. 530.) Not everyone lives to the same degree of righteousness on earth. Some live better or worse lives than others. Each person will inherit the degree of glory he earned while on the earth, according to his works, actions, behavior, and deeds. (See Revelation 22:11–22.)

PURPOSE OF THE WEEK

To learn about the degrees of glory in order to help us work toward the highest degree of the celestial kingdom, with exaltation and perfection as our ultimate goal.

SUNDAY

Purpose of the day: To learn about the mansions or kingdoms prepared by God. (Read John 14:2.)
Application: The world believes that there is only one heaven and one hell, and that all one has to do to get to heaven is to live a good life, and that to go to hell means one lives a bad life. The Lord has told us that there are many mansions or kingdoms prepared, and that each person will inherit that which he has merited on the earth. Today we will read and discuss this concept as explained in these scriptures: D&C 76; Psalm 73:24; 1 Corinthians 15:40–41; Revelation 22:11–12.

MONDAY

Purpose of the day: To learn about the celestial kingdom and the three degrees found there. (Read D&C 76:70; 131:1–2.)
Application: We will discuss with our family what the scriptures tell us about the celestial kingdom and will vow to attain this kingdom together. Hymns 109, "The Lord My Pasture Will Prepare," and 42, "Hail to the Brightness of Zion's Glad Morning," can add to the discussion.

TUESDAY

Purpose of the day: To learn more about the terrestrial and telestial kingdoms. (Read D&C 76:71, 81.)

Application: We will discuss the scriptures pertaining to these two kingdoms and will promise the Lord that we will work toward attaining the celestial kingdom and keeping the celestial law. Study of D&C 76:50–112 can help in our discussion.

WEDNESDAY

Purpose of the day: To learn that there is one kingdom which is without glory. (Read D&C 88:24.)

Application: We will discuss the reasons why some persons will inherit a kingdom without glory.

THURSDAY

Purpose of the day: To begin now to prepare ourselves to attain the celestial kingdom with its attendant glory. (Read D&C 14:7; 78:7; Revelation 3:21.)

Application: Several things are necessary for celestial preparation, including (1) receiving and honoring the priesthood (see D&C 84:35–39) and (2) standing behind, upholding, and encouraging the priesthood holders in our family. President Joseph Fielding Smith wrote: "Each kingdom, of course, is governed by laws. We have nothing to do with the laws of the telestial or terrestrial kingdom, so far as the preaching of the gospel is concerned. *Our mission is to preach the salvation of the kingdom of God* where he and Christ dwell, which is the celestial kingdom. And all of the principles of the gospel which have been given unto us pertain to the celestial kingdom." (*Doctrines of Salvation*, Bookcraft, 1955, vol. 2, pp. 25–26.) We will decide if we are doing the things we should be doing to obtain the celestial kingdom.

FRIDAY

Purpose of the day: To learn of some of the requirements necessary for obtaining exaltation and perfection. (Read 1 Peter 5:6; D&C 14:7; 76:5–6; Revelation 3:21.)

Application: The Lord has told us some of the requirements we must meet in order to obtain exaltation and perfection, including humility, being able to endure to the end, overcoming temptations and trials that come our way, and fearing, honoring, and serving the Lord. We will read the scriptures suggested above and will determine how we can develop positive attitudes toward overcoming our weaknesses and thus move in the direction of perfection and exaltation.

SATURDAY

Purpose of the day: To learn of the blessings that come to those who receive exaltation. (Read Romans 8:17; 1 Corinthians 2:9; D&C 132:17, 19, 20, 49.)

Application: We will read the scriptures listed above and will discuss the blessings that come with receiving eternal life and exaltation.

For additional scriptures see Topical Guide, "Exaltation."

Gaining a Divine Nature: Christlike Attributes

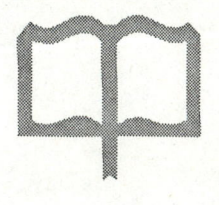

Love

29

The motive and the most dynamic force of the gospel of Jesus Christ is love.

DEFINITION
Love is the ultimate concern that brings about righteous service.

WHY LOVE?
Shakespeare said, "Love looks not with the eyes, but with the mind." Love is that emotion most esteemed by the Lord. According to some, it includes such feelings as reverence, tenderness, affection, and worship. this particular emotion helps people in their relationship with others, especially their relationship with God. Used wrongly or selfishly, this emotion can destroy relationships with others. Jesus said, "... thou shalt love the Lord thy God with all thy heart, and with all thy soul, and with all thy mind, and with all thy strength: this is the first commandment. And the second is like, namely this, Thou shalt love thy neighbour as thyself. There is none other commandment greater than these." (Mark 12:30–31.)

PURPOSE OF THE WEEK
To understand love and to make it a part of our lives.

SUNDAY
Purpose of the day: To learn to love God. (Read D&C 59:5.)
Application: We will each make a list of all the things God has done for us because he loves us. Then we will list what we will do this week to show our love. These scriptures can help us understand this concept: Matthew 22:37; John 14:15; 1 John 4:16; Deuteronomy 6:5.

MONDAY
Purpose of the day: To learn how we can love others. (Read Mosiah 4:15; 1 John 4:20–21.)
Application: We will discuss with our family how we can love others. Each family member will also tell how he can show love to another member of the family. Hymn 294, "Love at Home," can reinforce the discussion.

TUESDAY
Purpose of the day: To learn that love helps qualify us to do God's work. (Read D&C 12:8.)
Application: We will write down how love can help us specifically in doing God's work.

WEDNESDAY
Purpose of the day: To learn how love fulfills all the law. (Read Matthew 22:36–40.)
Application: Without love, nothing good could be accomplished. The power of love motivates many great things; it causes action, service, and all those behaviors which bring about good on the earth. We will write down at least three good things we know have been caused by love and then list the names of those whose love has helped bring these actions about.

THURSDAY

Purpose of the day: To learn how love is shown through service. (Read Galatians 5:13; Matthew 25:40.)

Application: We will discuss the importance of loving God first, our fellowmen second, and ourselves third. Then we will plan ways in which we can show our love to others through service.

FRIDAY

Purpose of the day: To learn to love our own family better. (Read Jacob 3:7; D&C 68:25–28.)

Application: The Lord has said that we should love our family, for the family is the basic unit in the Lord's kingdom. We will do something special for each member of our family and thus express our love for them.

SATURDAY

Purpose of the day: To learn of the rewards that come from loving God and others. (Read 4 Nephi 1:15.)

Application: Love of God and others not only brings peace in the land, but in our homes also. God has promised other blessings to those who love him and love others, including the gift of the Holy Ghost (D&C 76:116), eternal life (2 Nephi 31:20), prosperity (Psalm 122:6), the fact that we cannot do ill will to others (Romans 13:10), and that we will be known of God as a person of love (1 Corinthians 8:3). We will list which blessings we have already received through love and then promise that our love for God and for others will increase from this day forth.

For additional scriptures see Topical Guide, "Love"; "Charity."

Sacrifice

30

Denying oneself is a sign of a maturing and loving spirit. The ultimate goal is giving just as our Savior gave, the atoning sacrifice.

DEFINITION
Sacrifice means to surrender something desirable in behalf of a greater object, to give up something for a greater good.

WHY SACRIFICE?
Sacrifice is the ultimate test of the gospel. The Lord has asked his children to sacrifice in order to gain eternal life and exaltation. Without sacrifice, these goals are not attainable. According to Joseph Smith, "a religion that does not require the sacrifice of all things, never has power sufficient to produce the faith necessary unto life and salvation;... it is through... the sacrifice of all earthly things, that men do actually know that they are doing the things that are well pleasing in the sight of God." (Lecture on Faith, no. 6.)

PURPOSE OF THE WEEK

To see how sacrifice can help us gain salvation and eternal life.

SUNDAY

Purpose of the day: To learn that we must make sacrifices whenever the Lord asks us to do so. (Read D&C 97:8.)

Application: Making sacrifices for the Lord entails whatever we are asked: sacrifice of finances, of time, of talent, or of other things. It involves teaching classes, leading organizations, holding family home evening, preparing, working, doing. If Christ gave his life for us, shouldn't we give up just a bit of time, or money, or means, or talent for his sake? We will read and discuss the following scriptures on sacrifice: D&C 132:50; Psalm 4:5; Romans 12:1-2; Hebrews 10:26; 2 Nephi 2:7; and Alma 34:10-15.

MONDAY

Purpose of the day: To learn that one important sacrifice required by God is a broken heart and a contrite spirit. (Read 3 Nephi 9:20.)

Application: Having a broken heart and a contrite spirit implies being humble, repentant, willing to learn and serve, putting ourselves last and God first. We will discuss with our family having a broken heart and contrite spirit as sacrifices for the Lord. Hymn 131, "More Holiness Give Me," can help reinforce this concept.

TUESDAY

Purpose of the day: To learn that tithing is a sacrifice God requires of all men. (See D&C 97:12.)

Application: We will resolve to pay willingly not only our tithing, but all other financial obligations the Lord has asked, such as budget, welfare, and building fund. (Read D&C 64:23.)

WEDNESDAY

Purpose of the day: To learn that sometimes we must sacrifice everything for the gospel of Jesus Christ. (Read Matthew 19:29.)
Application: We will make a list of several sacrifices that we are willing to make for the Lord.

THURSDAY

Purpose of the day: To learn how doing good to others, often a sacrifice, is pleasing to God. (Read Hebrews 13:16.)
Application: The next time we are asked to participate in a welfare or service project, we will do so willingly and cheerfully.

FRIDAY

Purpose of the day: To learn that sacrifice must be done for the right reasons. (Read D&C 59:8.)
Application: We will pray that we will have the right spirit and attitude when we make sacrifices for the Lord.

SATURDAY

Purpose of the day: To learn that blessings come from making sacrifices. (Read D&C 132:55.)
Application: We will stop and think of the blessings we receive from making sacrifices for the Lord, both spiritual and temporal. In fact, as a reward, the Lord has said, "... and they who keep their second estate shall have glory added upon their heads for ever and ever." (Abraham 3:26.) Joseph Smith said that when the sacrifices, or sufferings, are over, "he will enter into eternal rest; and be a partaker of the glory of God." (Lecture on Faith, no. 6.) We will read or sing hymn 241, "Count Your Blessings," and think of all the blessings we receive because of sacrifice, especially the blessing of eternal life and salvation. (Read also Matthew 6:33.)

For additional scriptures see Topical Guide, "Sacrifice."

Obedience

31

Obedience is the first law of the gospel, the key to a righteous life.

DEFINITION
Obedience in an ecclesiastical sense means to follow the rule, guidance, or operation of Divinity. It includes being submissive to restraint, control, command, or jurisdiction.

WHY OBEDIENCE?
First, and foremost, obedience is necessary because it is a commandment of God. "There is a law, irrevocably decreed in heaven before the foundations of this world, upon which all blessings are predicated—And when we obtain any blessing from God, it is by obedience to that law upon which it is predicated." (D&C 130:20–21.) "And after many days an angel of the Lord appeared unto Adam, saying: Why dost thou offer sacrifice unto the Lord? And Adam said unto him: I know not, save the Lord commanded me." (Moses 5:6.) We cannot enter into the kingdom of God without obedience, for "obedience to God is the most infallible evidence of sincere and supreme love to him." (Emmons.)

PURPOSE OF THE WEEK
To become a more obedient person.

SUNDAY
Purpose of the day: To know that God wants us to be obedient. (Read Abraham 3:25.)
Application: We will read 2 Corinthians 10:5; 2 Nephi 27:13–22; and D&C 89:18, and then write down why obedience is important to us.

MONDAY
Purpose of the day: To learn that obedience shows that we love the Lord. (Read John 14:15.)
Application: Obedience and service are two ways of showing love to someone here on earth. Think how much greater is the need for these two things to show our love to our Father in heaven. We will read, in one of the Church magazines or a book by one of the General Authorities, an article or chapter on obedience, and will discuss it with our family. Hymn 237, "Do What Is Right," may help reinforce the concept of obedience.

TUESDAY
Purpose of the day: To learn that obedience should come first in life. (Read 1 Samuel 15:22 and 2 Nephi 28:8.)
Application: We will make a commitment to God that we will keep *all* of his commandments, not just those that we want to keep or those that can be seen by others.

WEDNESDAY
Purpose of the day: To learn that blessings come from obedience. (Read Mosiah 2:22 and Malachi 3:10.)
Application: We will thank the Lord in prayer for our many blessings.

THURSDAY

Purpose of the day: To learn that disobedience brings punishment. (Read D&C 105:6.)

Application: We will read the twelfth chapter of Alma, with particular emphasis on verses 16 and 17. Then we will ponder and discuss death, which is the greatest punishment God can mete out to those who are disobedient.

FRIDAY

Purpose of the day: To learn that we must set a good example of obedience. (Read Romans 5:19.)

Application: We will write down an example someone has set for us in righteousness and then write that person a letter of thanks for setting that good example.

SATURDAY

Purpose of the day: To remember the covenants of obedience made at the time of our baptism. (Mosiah 18:10.)

Application: We will reread the covenants we made at baptism and then will think of these covenants when we take the sacrament on Sunday.

For additional scriptures see Topical Guide, "Obedience"; "Righteous."

Gratitude

32

"How grateful our souls should be when we contemplate our surroundings and our wonderful opportunities!" (George Albert Smith, general conference, October 1946.)

DEFINITION
Gratitude, which means thankfulness, is an expression or acknowledgment for a favor or kindness received.

WHY GRATITUDE?
When we say "thank you" by word or deed, it is not only a polite expression, but it also shows our love and appreciation. Because the Lord has done so much, including giving us life here on earth, the gospel and plan of salvation, and the opportunity for exaltation, we ought to give him thanks for these many blessings. Gratitude gives rise to love, and love in action is righteous service.

PURPOSE OF THE WEEK
To count our many blessings and become more grateful for them.

Gaining a Divine Nature

SUNDAY

Purpose of the day: To show gratitude for God, for life on earth, and for our families. (Read Psalm 100:3–4.)
Application: We will read 2 Nephi 9:52; D&C 59:7; and Revelation 7:12. Then we will write a letter of thanks to our parents for their giving us birth.

MONDAY

Purpose of the day: To learn that singing is one way of saying thanks to God. (Read Psalm 95:1–2 and D&C 25:12.)
Application: With our family, we will sing or read the words of one of the following hymns: 94, "Come, Ye Thankful People"; 19, "We Thank Thee, O God, for a Prophet"; or 241, "When Upon Life's Billows." We will then discuss the blessings listed in the song.

TUESDAY

Purpose of the day: To show gratitude in prayer for *all* blessings, not just *some*. (Read D&C 46:32.)
Application: We will explain to a child how a prayer of thanksgiving is said. If we are not around a child to do this, we will write a letter to someone (preferably a child) explaining a prayer of thanksgiving.

WEDNESDAY

Purpose of the day: To learn that gratitude brings blessings. (Read D&C 78:19.)
Application: One writer has said, "Gratitude to God makes even a temporal blessing taste of heaven." (Romaine.) We will observe today how expressions of gratitude bring us happiness.

THURSDAY

Purpose of the day: To be grateful for the blessings of agency, of being able to choose right from wrong, of making choices in life. (Read 2 Nephi 2:16.)

Application: We will read 2 Nephi 2:26–27 and then write down why we appreciate having free agency from God.

FRIDAY

Purpose of the day: To learn gratitude for the blessing of God keeping his promises. (Read D&C 109:1.)
Application: We will visit a friend who is sick or troubled and help him to see that God always keeps his promises, no matter what the circumstances.

SATURDAY

Purpose of the day: To be thankful for our country. (Read Psalm 33:12.)
Application: We will tell the Lord that we appreciate the land in which we live and will then try to make our community a better one.

For additional scriptures see Topical Guide, "Ingratitude"; "Thanksgiving."

Kindness

33

"I expect to pass through this world but once; any good thing therefore that I can do, or any kindness that I can show to any fellow-creature, let me do it now; let me not defer or neglect it, for I shall not pass this way again." (Stephen Grellet.)

DEFINITION
Kindness is being benevolent and considerate, an act of good will.

WHY KINDNESS?
A kind word can turn away wrath, soothe an angered person, buoy up someone who is depressed, downhearted, or blue. A kind person is a peacemaker, one who truly loves his fellowmen and takes a genuine interest in another's welfare. Kindness can be given away; as the saying goes: "Smile and the world smiles with you; weep and you weep alone." Kindness goes with the smile; it brings love as its reward. President David O. McKay said, "(1) Look for the good in others. Focus on their strengths and not on their weaknesses—look for the

good in someone whom you may not like. (2) Think well of others. 'For as a man thinketh in his heart, so is he.' Try reading and contemplating 1 Corinthians each week until it becomes part of you. (3) Do something good for your 'enemies.' 'Do good to them that hate you.' "

PURPOSE OF THE WEEK

To make kindness an integral part of our life.

SUNDAY

Purpose of the day: To make all our decisions in kindness. (Read D&C 107:30.)
Application: We will write down a decision we have to make, considering how the decision will affect others around us. To help us make our decision with kindness toward others, we will read Joshua 2:12; Ephesians 4:32; Colossians 3:12; D&C 4:6.

MONDAY

Purpose of the day: To speak only kind words to others. (Read Proverbs 31:26.)
Application: We will discuss with our family the importance of using kind words, and will decide as a family that no matter what happens for one day, we will all speak only kind words. Hymns 232, "Let Us Oft Speak Kind Words," and 233, "Nay, Speak No Ill," can help reinforce this discussion.

TUESDAY

Purpose of the day: To remember the kindness of others. (Read Isaiah 54:10.)
Application: We will each write a letter to someone to thank that person for a specific kindness in the past.

WEDNESDAY

Purpose of the day: Kindness inspires trust, and trust returns kindness. (Read Psalm 36:7.)

Application: Elder Matthew Cowley once said, "My father never hesitated to place his hand in the hand of God. And that indeed was to him better than light and better than any known way." Kindness can inspire trust in one's self and trust in others. It can also inspire goodness and deeds of thoughtful consideration. We will write down one instance when we have been kind and mutual trust has resulted.

THURSDAY

Purpose of the day: To learn to always use kindness with discipline. (Read D&C 121:41–43.)
Application: If we must discipline someone this day, we will not lose our temper, but instead will use firmness and kindness.

FRIDAY

Purpose of the day: To learn that repayment of the Lord's kindness comes through kind deeds to others. (Read Isaiah 63:7.)
Application: The Lord has given us much in the way of kindness, including the gospel in all its glory. How do we return this loving kindness—by disobedience, unrighteousness, and iniquities, or by kindness, thoughtfulness, obedience, and righteous living? We will do a kind deed for someone with no thought of reward and without their knowing, if possible.

SATURDAY

Purpose of the day: To learn that kindness and love go hand in hand. (Read 2 Peter 1:7.)
Application: A person cannot become as God without having brotherly kindness and charity (or the pure love of Christ) in his heart. These three attributes—godliness, kindness, and charity—go one with another. We will try to love the Golden Rule completely for this one day.

For additional scriptures see Topical Guide, "Kindness."

Habits and Traditions
34

Man becomes and is what he thinks and does. Habit is the vehicle that molds his character.

DEFINITION
Habits are those customs or practices, aptitudes or inclinations for action that are acquired by repetition. A tradition is a belief, practice, custom, or information handed down by word of mouth; it is usually unwritten.

WHY HABITS AND TRADITIONS?
"Good habits are formed by acts of reason in persevering struggle with temptation." (Gilpin.) It takes work to form good habits. Bad ones are hard to break. Good habits and traditions can help us to keep the commandments of God, while bad ones help us to be disobedient. "Sow an act, and you reap a habit; sow a habit, and you reap a character; sow a character, and you reap a destiny." (George Dana Boardman.) What kind of character and destiny do we want? After all, actions should be the outgrowth of our beliefs.

PURPOSE OF THE WEEK

To cultivate good habits and to replace bad habits with good ones.

SUNDAY

Purpose of the day: To find out what good and bad habits we have. (Read D&C 93:39–40.)
Application: We will make a list of good and bad habits we learned as a child. Then we will know what work we have ahead of us. We will also read these additional scriptures: Alma 3:8, 11; D&C 89; Jeremiah 10:3; Luke 4:16.

MONDAY

Purpose of the day: To learn that bad habits must be replaced with good ones. (Read Alma 56:4.)
Application: We will discuss with our family replacing bad habits with good ones and have each person tell one good habit he would like to form and one bad one he would like to stop. Hymn 97, "Lead, Kindly Light," can help the discussion.

TUESDAY

Purpose of the day: To develop the good habit of Church attendance. (Read Moroni 6:5–6.)
Application: We will promise our Heavenly Father that we will faithfully attend sacrament meeting each week as well as all other meetings we should attend.

WEDNESDAY

Purpose of the day: To make a habit of keeping the Word of Wisdom. (Read D&C 89:1–2.)
Application: We will read section 89 of the Doctrine and Covenants and resolve to follow the instructions of the Lord as set forth in this Word of Wisdom.

THURSDAY

Purpose of the day: To make it a habit to follow righteous examples as portrayed in the scriptures, by Church leaders, in Church publications, etc. (Read Alma 37:9.)

Application: We will read two general conference talks from either the *Ensign* or *Conference Report*. What good or bad habits are implied in these two talks? We will make a good habit of reading the Church magazines regularly.

FRIDAY

Purpose of the day: To learn that repentance can help us overcome bad habits. (Read Helaman 5:51.)

Application: In our journals we will write down what repentance means to us and then list one bad habit that needs replacing.

SATURDAY

Purpose of the day: To learn that contention can be replaced by our becoming peacemakers. (Read 1 Corinthians 11:16.)

Application: Cheever said, "The habits of time are the soul's dress for eternity." We will commit ourselves to the Lord that we will try to be peacemakers at all times, that we will replace the habit of contention with peacemaking.

For additional scriptures see Topical Guide, "Family."

Attitude

35

"Success or failure in life is caused more by mental attitude than by mental capacities." (Author unknown.)

DEFINITION
Attitude is a feeling, a mood or "mental set," an outlook toward a person, a thing, or an idea. It is how a person feels or thinks inside himself as portrayed by his words and actions.

WHY ATTITUDE?
The attitude a person has will determine how he faces life and its problems, achievements, successes, and disappointments. In other words, attitude colors a person's complete outlook on everything. A positive, cheerful attitude can buoy a person up whatever the situation, the trial, the affliction, or the tribulation. He knows that God will never let him down, "for the Lord... forsaketh not his saints...." (Psalm 37:28.)

PURPOSE OF THE WEEK
To gain and put into practice a good attitude and outlook on life.

SUNDAY

Purpose of the day: To develop the habit of having positive thoughts. (Read Proverbs 23:7.)

Application: We will read the following scriptures: Psalm 40:17; Ecclesiastes 8:5; Matthew 9:4; Philippians 4:8; James 1:8; and Alma 56:47. Then for the whole day we will think nothing but positive, clean, wholesome thoughts about all things.

MONDAY

Purpose of the day: To have a positive, loving attitude toward God. (Read Alma 26:16.)

Application: We will read D&C 101:8 with our family and discuss having a positive attitude toward God. The following hymn can contribute to the discussion: 242, "Praise God, From Whom All Blessings Flow."

TUESDAY

Purpose of the day: To develop a more positive attitude toward ourselves and others. (Read 1 John 3:1.)

Application: We will write down why we must have a positive, yet humble, attitude about ourselves in order to have a good attitude toward others. We will read the following scriptures to help us: Proverbs 27:17; Matthew 9:2; Luke 10:29-37; John 15:13-14; 2 Nephi 10:23; Mosiah 24:15; D&C 68:6.

WEDNESDAY

Purpose of the day: To have a positive attitude about overcoming problems in life. (Read D&C 127:7-8.)

Application: We will do something cheerfully and willingly for someone who has more or greater problems than we have. (Read D&C 127:2.)

THURSDAY

Purpose of the day: To have a positive attitude about achieving goals in life. (Read 1 Nephi 17:17.)

Application: We will write down two goals on which we are actively working. (Read 1 Nephi 17:49–50 on Nephi's attitude.)

FRIDAY

Purpose of the day: To have a cheerful attitude about life. (Read 1 Nephi 3:5.)
Application: We will each write down several qualities we appreciate in another person and will try to integrate at least one of these qualities into our own lives.

SATURDAY

Purpose of the day: To have a positive attitude about repentance. (Read Alma 5:26.)
Application: We will each write down one attitude we have that needs changing and then work toward changing it.

For additional scriptures see Topical Guide, "Believe"; "Humility."

Courage, Diligence, Endurance

36

In applying true principles, work plus time equals success.

DEFINITIONS

Courage is that quality of mind, spirit, temper, or disposition that enables a person to meet danger and difficulties head-on with firmness, vigor, and valor. *Diligence* means to preserve and be industrious and painstaking. *Endurance* means to continue without perishing, to last, and to remain firm.

WHY COURAGE, DILIGENCE, AND ENDURANCE?

These three qualities—courage, diligence, and endurance—are necessary to keep the commandments of God. We must have the courage to follow our righteous convictions, diligence in keeping the commandments, and endurance so that we don't quit (even when that may be the easiest way). All three qualities are necessary in order to gain eternal life and exaltation.

PURPOSE OF THE WEEK

To understand courage, diligence, and endurance in their relation to the gospel, and to put them into our lives.

SUNDAY

Purpose of the day: To be courageous and diligent in keeping the commandments of God. (Read Joshua 22:5.)

Application: We will read Alma 34:32 (a time to prepare to meet God). Can we prepare without being courageous and diligent to the end? We will also read D&C 75:29 and 1 Nephi 4:34.

MONDAY

Purpose of the day: To learn that blessings come from enduring to the end courageously and diligently. (Read D&C 14:7.)

Application: We will discuss with our family the blessings that come from enduring to the end. Hymn 3, "Now Let Us Rejoice," and the following scriptures can help reinforce the discussion: Deuteronomy 31:6; 1 Nephi 2:19–20; 2 Nephi 10:17, 19; Moroni 8:26; D&C 101:36–38; D&C 121:29.

TUESDAY

Purpose of the day: To learn how to use courage and diligence in magnifying our callings. (Read Jacob 2:3.)

Application: We will resolve to be more diligent in magnifying our callings. We will make a list of things to do, with completion dates for each item.

WEDNESDAY

Purpose of the day: To be diligent and courageous in teaching others. (Read D&C 88:78.)

Application: We will list ways in which we can be courageous in teaching and in setting a good example.

THURSDAY

Purpose of the day: To be diligent and courageous in learning and studying. (Read D&C 88:118.)
Application: We will read D&C 130:19 and Mosiah 1:7 and then set up a study schedule for each day.

FRIDAY

Purpose of the day: To be diligent and courageous in listening to God. (Read 2 Nephi 9:51.)
Application: The word of God has great power, and if we are obedient, it can save us. We will make an effort to listen to the Spirit throughout the day and to follow his promptings.

SATURDAY

Purpose of the day: To do temple work and genealogical research diligently and courageously. (Read D&C 127:4.)
Application: We will set definite goals for doing genealogical research and temple work, and will begin to work toward these goals.

For additional scriptures see Topical Guide, "Courage"; "Diligence"; "Endure."

Courtesy and Manners
37

"There is a courtesy of the heart; it is allied to love. —From it springs the purest courtesy in the outward behavior." (Goethe.)

DEFINITION
Courtesy means performing favors with kindness and respect and politeness. *Manners* include the way we act, how we proceed—in fact, all our normal behavior.

WHY COURTESY AND MANNERS?
Courtesy and manners pave the road of life with sweetness and kindness. They are how we help others, how we live in our relationships with other people. They include putting others before ourselves.

PURPOSE OF THE WEEK
To become more courteous and mannerly in our relations with others.

SUNDAY

Purpose of the day: To learn what the scriptures teach us about being courteous. (Read 1 Peter 3:8.)

Application: We will read the following scriptures on being kind, gentle, and courteous to others: Acts 27:3; Acts 28:7; James 3:17; and D&C 121:41. Then we will write down five ways in which each of us can be extra courteous to members of our family this week. We will check up on ourselves at the end of the week.

MONDAY

Purpose of the day: To learn that thoughtlessness breeds discourtesy. (Read Alma 60:6.)

Application: We will discuss courtesy and good manners with our family. Each person should state one way in which he can be courteous to others. Hymn 228, "If There's Sunshine in Your Heart," can encourage courteous behavior.

TUESDAY

Purpose of the day: To learn how thoughts and words contribute to good or bad manners. (Read 1 Corinthians 15:33.)

Application: If we think and speak kindly, courteously, and gently, then our actions will be courteous. If we think and speak in an evil manner or are grumpy, impolite, or indifferent, then our actions will follow suit. For one day we will think about courtesy and speak courteously to everyone with whom we come in contact.

WEDNESDAY

Purpose of the day: To learn to follow the Spirit, which will direct us in being more courteous. (Read D&C 82:9.)

Application: If we are in tune and will listen, the Spirit will indicate to us how we should behave toward others. We will commit ourselves to following the Spirit in all our actions and behavior.

THURSDAY

Purpose of the day: To learn that courtesy and good manners include respect for the law. (Read D&C 134:6.)

Application: Respecting the law includes courtesy to others, especially when we are behind the wheel of an automobile. We will resolve that we will be courteous with respect to the laws of the land, especially while in an automobile.

FRIDAY

Purpose of the day: To learn that courtesy and good manners should be extended to everyone. (Read Acts 28:7.)

Application: For this one day, we will be courteous to everyone, no matter how they react to us. We will try to make this a habit for every day.

SATURDAY

Purpose of the day: To learn that our inner self is depicted by our actions. (Read Proverbs 23:7.)

Application: President Joseph F. Smith said, "No man is safe unless he is master of himself." (*Elders Journal*, vol. 4, p. 271.) We will evaluate ourselves to see if our good manners are surface manners or a part of our character. Then we will check up to see if we have followed through on the five areas of courtesy and good manners we selected on Sunday.

For additional scriptures see Topical Guide, "Courtesy"; "Kindness"; "Reverence."

Humility

38

True greatness and the ability to be an instrument in the hands of God depend upon acquiring humility.

DEFINITION
Humility means freedom from pride and arrogance, from being pretentious or puffed up. To be humble is to be teachable and unassuming.

WHY HUMILITY?
Humility is the first step toward salvation. Without it, nothing can be accomplished. Brigham Young said, "Let us be humble, fervent, submissive, yielding ourselves to the will of the Lord, and there is no danger but that we shall have his Spirit to guide us." (*Journal of Discourses,* vol. 13, p. 155.) "True humility is *not* an abject, groveling, self-despising spirit; it is but a right estimate of ourselves as God sees us." (Tryon Edwards.) "Nothing sets a person so much out of the devil's reach as humility." (Jonathan Edwards.)

PURPOSE OF THE WEEK
To learn to become humble.

SUNDAY

Purpose of the day: To learn that appreciation of God's creations can help make a person humble. (Read Moses 1:8, 10.)
Application: We will read Moses, chapter 1. Then we will look at something God has created—such as a flower, a tree, a rock, a mountain, a meadow, a lake—to see God's greatness and learn humility through his creations. We will read Acts 20:19; Alma 13:28; Ether 12:27; D&C 112:10.

MONDAY

Purpose of the day: To learn how humility and repentance work together. (Read Mosiah 4:10.)
Application: With our family, we will discuss the meaning and application of repentance. (Read 3 Nephi 9:20.) Hymn 172, "In Humility, Our Savior," can help us implement this concept in our lives.

TUESDAY

Purpose of the day: To learn that one aspect of humility is being as a little child. (Read Matthew 18:4.)
Application: We will list the humble attributes of a child and begin to acquire them in our daily lives.

WEDNESDAY

Purpose of the day: To learn of the blessings that come from humility. (Read D&C 1:28.)
Application: We will list several blessings that can come from humility.

THURSDAY

Purpose of the day: To learn that humility comes from learning of God and his attributes. (Read D&C 67:10.)
Application: We will read D&C 67:10 daily and try to know God.

FRIDAY

Purpose of the day: To learn to study with prayer and humility. (Read D&C 136:32.)

Application: We will evaluate our study schedule for reading the scriptures, knowing that if we are humble in this, we will learn through the Holy Spirit.

SATURDAY

Purpose of the day: To learn that pride, the opposite of humility, can prevent entry into the kingdom of God. (Read Proverbs 16:18.)

Application: We will write down the many things we have that come from God.

For additional scriptures see Topical Guide, "Humility"; "Contrite Heart"; "Meek"; "Submissiveness"; "Teachable."

Integrity and Sincerity
39

Honesty and sincerity of self make our actions acceptable before God.

DEFINITION
Integrity means being of moral soundness, honesty, and uprightness. *Sincerity* means being honest with ourselves in our actions and in our words. A person with sincerity and integrity is complete, undivided, and unbroken in his morality, free from hypocrisy and dissimulation, real and genuine. This person is pure in his motives.

WHY INTEGRITY AND SINCERITY?
"Give us the man of integrity, on whom we know we can thoroughly depend; who will stand firm when others fail; the friend, faithful and true; the adviser, honest and fearless; the adversary, just and chivalrous; such an one is a fragment of the Rock of Ages." (A. P. Stanley.) The whole of a person's moral character is focused in his integrity and sincerity. If he has these qualities, there is no room for guile, deceit, and evil. These qualities bring trust, love, belief, and friendship. This

person lives what he says and teaches. He is no hypocrite, saying one thing and doing another. "Sincerity and truth are the basis of every virtue." (Confucius.)

PURPOSE OF THE WEEK
To make integrity and sincerity a part of our lives.

SUNDAY
Purpose of the day: To discover what sincere integrity is. (Read D&C 124:15.)
Application: We will write in our journals each of the characteristics included in integrity and sincerity (from the definition). We will state how we can improve in each area. At the end of the week we will evaluate ourselves to measure our progress. (Read also Alma 27:27; Helaman 9:36; 2 Nephi 9:34.)

MONDAY
Purpose of the day: To learn that we must be sincere and honest in word and deed. (Read Isaiah 29:13.)
Application: We will discuss with our family sincerity and integrity. Hymn 254, "True to the Faith," can help reinforce today's purpose.

TUESDAY
Purpose of the day: To set a proper example of honesty and sincerity. (Read Proverbs 20:7.)
Application: We will each write a thank-you letter to someone who has set an example of honesty and sincerity for us or to someone who helped teach us these principles.

WEDNESDAY
Purpose of the day: To be sincere and honest in loving Jesus Christ and our fellowmen. (Read Ephesians 6:24.)
Application: We will each perform an honest, sincere service for someone without being asked to do so. Then we will read Philippians 4:8.

THURSDAY

Purpose of the day: To learn that we must be governed by sincere, honest people. (Read D&C 98:10.)

Application: At the time of the next election— school, club, local, state, etc.—we will find out about those running for office, learn what they stand for, and become involved. Then we will vote our conscience.

FRIDAY

Purpose of the day: To set honest and sincere standards. (Read Proverbs 11:3.)

Application: When we have a decision to make, we will consider whether or not it is right for us according to the goals we have set and according to what our Heavenly Father wants us to do (not whether or not it will please our neighbors or our friends). Then we will make our decision and do the will of Heavenly Father.

SATURDAY

Purpose of the day: To learn that we can retain the characteristics of honesty and sincerity, no matter what happens. (Read Job 2:3.)

Application: We will evaluate our progress in attaining sincerity and integrity in our everyday life and then resolve to retain these characteristics always. We will make our commitment to the Lord today—forever.

For additional scriptures see Topical Guide, "Honesty."

Loyalty

40

"Nothing is more noble, nothing more venerable than fidelity." (Cicero.)

DEFINITION
Loyalty means being faithful to the lawful government or sovereign (religious or secular) to whom one is subject. It also means being true and devoted to a person to whom one owes fidelity.

WHY LOYALTY?
If a person is loyal to his Heavenly Father and his precepts, he is constant in his allegiance. He does not deviate from the course outlined by the Lord. Being loyal to God includes loyalty to fellowmen. A person cannot be false to anyone when he is loyal to his God. "Among the faithless, faithful only he: / Among innumerable false, unmoved, / Unshaken, unseduced, unterrified / His loyalty he kept, his love, his zeal." (John Milton, *Paradise Lost,* Book 5.)

PURPOSE OF THE WEEK

To become a more loyal person by learning of and putting loyalty into our life.

SUNDAY

Purpose of the day: To learn that loyalty to God means that one cannot serve two masters. (Read Matthew 6:24.)
Application: We will read Jacob 2:17–19, 3 Nephi 13:33, Mark 3:25, and Matthew 12:25, and then write down how loyalty is implied in these scriptures.

MONDAY

Purpose of the day: To learn that loyalty denotes action. (Read D&C 27:18.)
Application: We will discuss with our family how we can be active in our loyalties to the Lord and to our community. Hymn 239, "Choose the Right," can help reinforce the discussion.

TUESDAY

Purpose of the day: To learn to be loyal to the counsel of God. (Read D&C 124:13.)
Application: We will write down one or more ways in which we can show loyalty to our Father in heaven and to the leaders of the Church.

WEDNESDAY

Purpose of the day: To learn that loyalty brings blessings from God. (Read Alma 38:2.)
Application: As a continuation of Tuesday's application, we will list one or more blessings we can receive for being loyal to God and to the leaders of the Church.

THURSDAY

Purpose of the day: To show loyalty in filling responsibilities and callings. (Read Nehemiah 7:2.)

Application: We will each make a verbal commitment to the Lord that we will be loyal in our service to him by fulfilling our responsibilities in the Church to the best of our ability.

FRIDAY

Purpose of the day: To learn to be loyal to our friends. (Read 2 Nephi 1:30.)
Application: We will tell a loyal friend how much we appreciate his friendship.

SATURDAY

Purpose of the day: To learn to be loyal to our country. (Read Alma 62:37.)
Application: We will write a letter to a serviceman from our ward or branch and tell him how much we appreciate his serving to help keep our country free.

For additional scriptures see Topical Guide, "Loyalty."

Self-Control

41

"Let us resolve that we shall practice more self-control in our homes, control our tempers and our tongues, and control our feelings, that they may not wander beyond the bounds of right and purity, more seeking the presence of God, realizing how dependent we are upon him for success in this life, and particularly for success in the positions we hold in the Church." (David O. McKay, general conference address, April 1952.)

DEFINITION
Self-control means control of oneself; limiting, directing, guiding, and/or restraining oneself.

WHY SELF-CONTROL?
How can we ever learn, teach, serve, or become as God if we cannot control ourselves? As John Locke said, "The most precious of all possessions is power over ourselves; power to withstand trial, to bear suffering, to front danger; power over

pleasure and pain; power to follow our convictions, however resisted by menace and scorn; the power of calm reliance in scenes of darkness and storms. He that has not a mastery over his inclinations; he that knows not how to resist the importunity of present pleasure or pain, for the sake of what reason tells him is fit to be done, wants the true principle of virtue and industry, and is in danger of never being good for anything."

PURPOSE OF THE WEEK

To work on strengthening our self-control.

SUNDAY

Purpose of the day: To set self-control as a standard and goal in our lives. (Read Titus 1:7–8.)
Application: We will read D&C 12:8 and Alma 7:23 to learn some of the good traits self-control can help us attain. Then we will set a goal to develop self-control in our lives.

MONDAY

Purpose of the day: To start to control our time better. (Read Luke 15:13.)
Application: With our family, we will discuss how many hours we spend watching TV and the types of programs we watch. Then each family member will resolve to take part of that TV time and spend it two ways (setting up a flexible schedule): (1) on a hobby and/or talent, and (2) reading the scriptures. Read the words to hymn 232, "Let Us Oft Speak Kind Words."

TUESDAY

Purpose of the day: To begin to control a passion, urge, or bad trait. (Read Alma 38:12.)
Application: We will read Proverbs 16:32, and then write down a trait we wish to control; for example, our tempers. Then we will begin to follow through and control that trait.

WEDNESDAY

Purpose of the day: To learn to control our tongues. (Read D&C 88:121.)

Application: We will post the scripture mentioned above in a prominent place in our home (on the bathroom mirror, the refrigerator door, etc.) so we can see it and refer to it often. Then for one day, we will make a special effort to say nothing bad about anyone.

THURSDAY

Purpose of the day: To set high standards and control base urges. (Read 1 John 2:16.)

Application: We *are* what we *like*. We will resolve to set and hold our standards high; to think clean thoughts for a whole day, then a week, then continually.

FRIDAY

Purpose of the day: To learn to control our wants. (Read D&C 101:6; 2 Nephi 9:51.)

Application: We will make a list of things we want, by priority, and then put a check beside those really worth working for. We will cross out the ones that won't really make our life worthwhile.

SATURDAY

Purpose of the day: To learn about the Word of Wisdom and how it helps us develop self-control. (Read D&C 89:4.)

Application: We will read the promise given in D&C 89:18–21 for those who follow the Word of Wisdom, and promise the Lord that we will keep this commandment.

For additional scriptures see Topical Guide, "Self-mastery."

Self-Esteem

42

"Those lacking in that important understanding [Who am I?], and consequently, in some degree [those] failing to hold themselves in the high esteem which they would have if they did understand, are lacking self-respect." (Harold B. Lee, general conference, October 1973.)

DEFINITION

Self-esteem means self-respect, self-approval, and self-confidence. It is a realization of the kind of person each of us is and also the kind of person we can become.

WHY SELF-ESTEEM?

What a wonderful thing it is to be a human being, a person, a son or daughter of God. This knowledge brings self-esteem, and with self-esteem, we acknowledge our faults but take a confident approach to life and ourselves. A person cannot respect himself without knowing himself. With this knowledge comes positive action—self-mastery and self-control.

PURPOSE OF THE WEEK

To gain greater self-esteem through knowledge and understanding.

SUNDAY

Purpose of the day: To learn how knowledge that each person is a child of God can increase one's self-esteem. (Read Romans 8:16.)

Application: We will read and discuss the following scriptures as they relate to being a child of God: Luke 20:36; Galatians 3:26; 1 John 3:10; Mosiah 18:22; D&C 58:51.

MONDAY

Purpose of the day: To learn how knowledge of ourselves can increase self-esteem. (Read D&C 38:24–25.)

Application: Before we can love others as ourselves, we must first know and love ourselves. We will discuss the goodness of each person in the family so that each might realize his own self-worth. Hymns 292, "O My Father," and 301, "I Am a Child of God," can all be related to self-esteem.

TUESDAY

Purpose of the day: To learn how knowing we are created in God's image can increase self-esteem. (Read Genesis 1:26–27.)

Application: Each of us looks a lot like our parents. We are also created in the image of our Heavenly Father. Think what a blessing this is: to know that we have a Heavenly Father, that he loves us, and that he created us like himself, and that we can become as he is if we live righteously. We will tell our parents, either verbally or in writing, how much we appreciate them, and help them to see their self-worth through our words of appreciation and gratitude.

WEDNESDAY

Purpose of the day: To learn how knowledge of human life itself can increase self-esteem. (Read Abraham 3:22–23.)

Application: Man is truly a wonderful creation of God—complicated in structure, in organization, in mental abilities and intelligence, and in spirituality. We will live up to our potential this day and do our best in all we do.

THURSDAY

Purpose of the day: To learn how knowing our strengths and weaknesses can increase self-esteem. (Read 1 Kings 3:5, 7, 9.)
Application: We will each make a chart of our strengths, including our talents and weaknesses so that we might know ourselves better. Then we will make a plan of action for self-improvement.

FRIDAY

Purpose of the day: To learn how service to God can increase our self-esteem. (Read Mosiah 23:10–11.)
Application: We will covenant with our Heavenly Father that we will do our best to make an accurate estimate of ourselves so that he might make good use of us and our talents in his service.

SATURDAY

Purpose of the day: To learn how knowing that God loves us can increase our self-esteem. (Read Psalm 8:4–5.)
Application: We will thank our Father in heaven for creating us, for loving us, and for giving us the chance to become like him.

For additional scriptures see Topical Guide, "Man, a Spirit Child of Heavenly Father"; "Man, Potential to Become like Heavenly Father"; "Worth of Souls."

Tolerance and Patience
43

"Patience strengthens the spirit, sweetens the temper, stifles anger, extinguishes envy, subdues pride, bridles the tongue, restrains the hand, and tramples upon temptations." (George Horne.)

DEFINITIONS
Tolerance means to allow, to permit beliefs, practices, or habits differing from one's own. It includes forbearance. *Patience* is to bear or endure pains, trials, etc., without complaints, with long-suffering and forbearance.

WHY TOLERANCE AND PATIENCE?
In order to get through life on earth, our mortal existence, we must be patient. This is the time of trials and tribulations, when we learn to endure come what may. Gaining tolerance and patience can help us along the path toward eternal life and exaltation.

PURPOSE OF THE WEEK
To learn about and practice tolerance and patience.

SUNDAY

Purpose of the day: To be tolerant of those whose religious beliefs are different. (Read Article of Faith 11.)

Application: We will compare another person's religious beliefs to the teachings of the gospel so that we might be more understanding of that person. Reading the following scriptures will help us better understand tolerance: Romans 15:4–5; 3 Nephi 12:38–42; D&C 134:12.

MONDAY

Purpose of the day: To learn to bear with the shortcomings of others in our personal relationships. (Read D&C 42:43.)

Application: We will discuss with our family the difference between tolerance of the sinner and intolerance of the sin. Then we will discuss having patience in overcoming imperfections. Hymn 239, "Choose the Right," can help reinforce the discussion.

TUESDAY

Purpose of the day: To learn that the Lord will not tolerate sin. (Read Alma 45:16.)

Application: We have been told that no unclean thing can dwell with the Lord. We will make a commitment to him that we will repent of our sins, and will help others to make this same commitment.

WEDNESDAY

Purpose of the day: To learn that the Lord asks patience of everyone for all things. (Read Mosiah 23:21.)

Application: We will make an effort to be patient for one whole day, no matter what happens. We will not lose our tempers or speak angry words.

THURSDAY

Purpose of the day: To learn that patience includes turning the other cheek. (Read Matthew 5:39.)

Application: We will discuss what it means to turn the other cheek and will set an example of patience and kindness in this regard.

FRIDAY

Purpose of the day: To learn that perfection can come with patience. (Read D&C 67:13.)

Application: The Lord rewards those who, with patience and work, endure to the end. We will write down three traits we want to develop in order to become more perfect. We know we must not expect perfection immediately; but with hard work and patience, perfection will come eventually.

SATURDAY

Purpose of the day: To learn that blessings come from patience. (Read D&C 101:38.)

Application: As a continuation of Friday's application, we will make out a schedule for working on the three traits toward perfection.

For additional scriptures see Topical Guide, "Patience"; "Forbear"; "Understanding."

Virtue, Chastity, Modesty

44

"Virtue is its own reward, and brings with it the truest and highest pleasure." (John Henry Newman.)

DEFINITION
Virtue, chastity, and modesty mean being chaste, pure, and moral in thought and action. They also include absence of self-assertion, arrogance, or presumption.

WHY VIRTUE, CHASTITY, AND MODESTY?
The Lord has said that no unclean thing can dwell in his presence. By practicing virtue, chastity, and modesty, we can remain clean and pure; thus we can eventually come into the Lord's presence.

PURPOSE OF THE WEEK
To strive to keep virtue, chastity, and modesty in our lives.

SUNDAY
Purpose of the day: To learn that virtue is most precious in God's sight. (Read Moroni 9:9.)

Application: The Lord has said that those holding his priesthood must be clean (D&C 38:42) and that women must be virtuous and clean (Jacob 2:28; Proverbs 12:4; and Proverbs 31:10). We will write down the ways in which a person can be clean, pure, virtuous, chaste, and modest.

MONDAY

Purpose of the day: To learn that God looks on the sex sin as abominable. (Read Alma 39:5.)
Application: We will discuss with our family what virtue, chastity, and modesty mean. Hymn 157, "Thy Spirit, Lord, Has Stirred Our Souls," can contribute to the discussion.

TUESDAY

Purpose of the day: To learn that virtue is necessary for temple marriage. (Read D&C 131:1–2.)
Application: We will read D&C 132 and determine if we are living worthy of celestial marriage.

WEDNESDAY

Purpose of the day: To learn that breaking the commandment of virtue and chastity brings unhappiness. (Read Alma 41:10.)
Application: We will make a list of specific problems that arise from being unchaste.

THURSDAY

Purpose of the day: To learn that blessings come from being virtuous. (Read D&C 25:2.)
Application: We will make a list of the *temporal* blessings that come from virtuous living.

FRIDAY

Purpose of the day: To make all our thoughts clean and virtuous. (Read D&C 121:45.)
Application: Christ said that even having thoughts of lust is a sin and as bad as committing the sin itself. (See Matthew 5:27–

28.) For this day we will keep our thoughts absolutely clean and then strive to continue this pattern in the future.

SATURDAY

Purpose of the day: To learn that each of us is a temple of God and that we should keep our temple clean. (Read D&C 93:35; 1 Corinthians 6:19.)

Application: We will make a commitment to God that from this day forward we will be clean in every way: in word, thought, and deed.

For additional scriptures see Topical Guide, "Virtue"; "Chastity"; "Modesty"; "Purity."

Envy, Strife, Backbiting, Selfishness, Contention

45

"Nay, speak no ill; a kindly word can never leave a sting behind; and, oh, to breathe each tale we've heard is far beneath a noble mind." (Hymns, no. 233.)

DEFINITIONS

Envy means being upset and/or discontented with the excellence or good fortune of another person (or several others). It includes being resentful and begrudging; longing for, desiring, and coveting those things that others have. *Strife* means working or contending for superiority; it includes emulation, altercation, conflict, and discord. *Backbiting* means to speak evil of or to gossip about one who is not present; to slander another person. *Selfishness* means caring too much for oneself, regarding one's own comfort and advantages at the expense of and disregard for those of others. *Contention* means to strive in opposition; it includes rivalry, argumentation, controversy, altercation, quarreling, and disputing.

WHY RESIST ENVY, STRIFE, BACKBITING, SELFISHNESS, AND CONTENTION?

Envy, strife, backbiting, selfishness, and contention are tools of the devil and can lead a person away from the path of truth down toward hell. These qualities cause people to fall away from the Church, to stop being true Christians, to stop living the kind of life that will lead them to eternal life and exaltation. They are against the commandments of God. As the poet says,

> Vice is a monster of so frightful mein,
> As to be hated needs but to be seen;
> Yet seen too oft, familiar with her face,
> We first endure, then pity, then embrace.
> —Alexander Pope

Are we willing to jeopardize our exaltation for a petty vice, one that doesn't *seem* to be too bad? Yet these so-called "petty vices" are the very ones that can lead to destruction.

PURPOSE OF THE WEEK

To see what the petty vices can do to people to lead them from the path of righteousness, and to help us begin to rout them out of our own characters.

SUNDAY

Purpose of the day: To understand that the "natural man" who doesn't follow God's commandments and who doesn't repent is an enemy to God, and to understand that we should stop our vices and begin to be more humble, contrite, and loving. (Read Mosiah 3:19.)

Application: We will evaluate ourselves on each of the five vices—envy, strife, backbiting, selfishness, and contention—and will begin to eliminate them from our daily lives. We will check up on ourselves at the end of the week.

MONDAY

Purpose of the day: To eliminate envy from our lives. (Read Galatians 5:21.)

Application: We will discuss envy and the other topics of the week with our family and determine that all family members should eliminate these qualities from their lives and strive to keep them out. The following hymns can help reinforce this idea: 235, "Should You Feel Inclined to Censure"; 240, "Know This, That Every Soul Is Free"; 237, "Do What Is Right"; 116, "Come, Follow Me."

TUESDAY

Purpose of the day: To eliminate strife from our lives. (Read D&C 101:6.)

Application: For one day, we will each live in peace and agreement with those around us, not cause any friction or strife, and try to see the other person's point of view.

WEDNESDAY

Purpose of the day: To eliminate backbiting from our lives. (Read D&C 20:54.)

Application: For one day, we will make a conscious effort not to talk about anyone. If we must talk about a person, we will say only those things that are good, kind, and praiseworthy of that person.

THURSDAY

Purpose of the day: To eliminate selfishness from our lives. (Read Proverbs 21:26.)

Application: We will give something away to someone who needs it without that person knowing who gave it to them.

FRIDAY

Purpose of the day: To eliminate contention from our lives. (Read 3 Nephi 11:29.)

Application: For this one day we will not quarrel or argue with anyone about anything.

SATURDAY

Purpose of the day: To make a choice as to the kinds of qualities we want in our character. (Read Helaman 14:30.)

Application: We will check up on our progress in regard to envy, strife, backbiting, selfishness, and contention, and resolve to keep working to remove them from our characters.

For additional scriptures see "Envy"; "Covet"; "Jealous"; "Selfishness"; "Contention.".

Criticism and Judging
46

To criticize and judge unrighteously is damning to the person who indulges in this practice.

DEFINITION
To be critical and judging means to criticize, to censure, to conclude or decide, to suppose, to talk about others in a critical or disapproving manner, to find fault, to tear down. Criticism and/or judgment is usually negative rather than positive in nature.

WHY STOP BEING CRITICAL AND JUDGING?
President David O. McKay said that Latter-day Saints should be critical of evil conditions that exist in the world, but they should not "revile the character of men." He went on to say that "there is a trait in the heart of the world to pick at their fellow-men." (General conference address, April 1910.) This tendency should be discouraged and not encouraged. We should help others overcome their problems, not push them deeper in the mire through adverse criticism and judgment. And ofttimes we tend to overlook in our own character those faults we

criticize in others. Then too, when we judge another, we are trying to lower others so we will be higher. This is not how the Lord expects us to act.

PURPOSE OF THE WEEK
To eliminate criticism and judgment of others from our lives.

SUNDAY
Purpose of the day: To learn that the Lord says we are not to judge others. (Read Matthew 7:1.)
Application: We will read the following scriptures on judging and fault-finding: Psalm 34:13; Luke 6:37; 3 Nephi 14:1–5; Matthew 7:1–5; Mormon 8:19–20; and Moroni 7:14. Then we will resolve that we will refrain from criticizing other people.

MONDAY
Purpose of the day: To learn that our judgment of others will bring this same judgment upon ourselves. (Read 3 Nephi 14:2.)
Application: We will read Romans 2:1 and compare Matthew 7:2 with 3 Nephi 14:2; then we will discuss fault-finding and criticizing with our family. Hymns 233, "Nay, Speak No Ill," and 273, "Truth Reflects upon Our Senses," can help reinforce the concept of the day.

TUESDAY
Purpose of the day: If the Lord asks us to make judgments or evaluations, we must make them in righteousness. (Read Moroni 7:18.)
Application: There are some positions in the Church where evaluations and judgments must be made, such as that of bishop. When an evaluation or judgment must be made, it should be done in righteousness. Are we humble and righteous enough to make this type of judgment when required? We will read D&C 107, especially verses 72–76, about judging in righteousness. Alma 41:14 and D&C 121:43 can also help us learn how righteous judgment is made.

WEDNESDAY

Purpose of the day: To learn that a person must look to his own self before he can criticize another. (Read Matthew 7:3–5.)

Application: We will each write down one fault we are prone to criticize in another person and see if it is a fault we have in our own character. Then we will resolve not to judge or criticize another person for this fault.

THURSDAY

Purpose of the day: To learn that because we cannot always tell the wicked from the righteous; and because we don't always know the reasons for another's actions, we should not judge others. (Read D&C 10:37.)

Application: For this one day, we will not criticize or judge anyone for anything they do or say. We will make up a good reason for their actions and give them the benefit of every doubt.

FRIDAY

Purpose of the day: To learn that vengeance belongs to the Lord, not to man. (Read Mormon 8:20 and D&C 29:17.)

Application: The Lord says that vengeance is his. We are to be loving and kind, and he will take care of the other person. The next time we want to "hit back" when we are "wronged" or "hurt," we will think of the above scriptures and be loving and kind instead. (Read also Romans 12:17–19.)

SATURDAY

Purpose of the day: To realize that God will judge perfectly, and we are to live perfectly. (Read D&C 64:11.)

Application: We will promise the Lord that we will try to live more perfectly and leave the judging to him.

For additional scriptures see Topical Guide, "Chastening"; "Murmuring"; "Judgment."

Covenant Making and Sustaining Our Leaders

47

Covenant making is the divine method of obedience, the key to all blessings.

DEFINITION
A covenant is an agreement, pact, promise, or contract between people, or between man and God. Sustaining means to support, bear up, furnish sustenance for, aid effectively, hold valid, and uphold.

WHY COVENANT MAKING AND SUSTAINING OUR LEADERS?
Covenants are the agreements we make with God. He is bound by them, and our blessings are dependent upon them. When we sustain our leaders, we take action or make a motion that is binding on ourselves, and we commit ourselves to support those people whom we have sustained.

PURPOSE OF THE WEEK

To learn about making covenants with the Lord and keeping them, and to learn about sustaining the leaders of the Church, so that we may do both in our lives.

SUNDAY

Purpose of the day: To learn that we must be willing to enter into covenants with the Lord. (Read Mosiah 5:5.)
Application: We will write down two covenants we have made with God, and will read these scriptures about covenants and covenant making: Genesis 9:15; Psalm 105:8–11; Mosiah 18:13; Mosiah 24:13; D&C 25:13; D&C 33:14.

MONDAY

Purpose of the day: To learn that the Lord keeps his promises when we keep our covenants with him. (Read D&C 82:10.)
Application: A covenant is a two-way street. If we keep our end of the bargain, then the Lord will keep his. However, if we do not keep our part, then the Lord is not bound to keep his. We will make a commitment to the Lord that from this day forth all covenants made (past, present, and future) will be kept. We will help our family members to make this same commitment. Hymn 91, "Father, Thy Children to Thee Now Raise," can help us remember this principle.

TUESDAY

Purpose of the day: To learn that curses follow the breaking of covenants, and blessings come with keeping them. (Read D&C 35:24; 104:5–6.)
Application: We will list the specific curses and blessings in regard to disobedience to the following covenants: baptism, gift of the Holy Ghost, and temple marriage.

WEDNESDAY

Purpose of the day: To learn that we must repent before we can make a covenant with the Lord. (Read 2 Nephi 30:2; Alma 7:15.)

Application: The Lord will not make covenants with those who are not repentant. We will promise the Lord that we will repent so that we might keep the covenants we have made with him.

THURSDAY

Purpose of the day: To learn that the people of the Church are to acknowledge and sustain the prophet of the Church. (Read D&C 102:9.)
Application: Sustaining the prophet means that we uphold him and will follow the directives he gives to the Church. We will make a solemn vow that we will sustain the prophet of the Lord from this time forth.

FRIDAY

Purpose of the day: To learn that when we sustain the prophet, we are sustaining the Lord. (Read D&C 21:4–5.)
Application: We will write down what it means to sustain the prophet and thus sustain the Lord.

SATURDAY

Purpose of the day: To learn that leaders of the various wards, branches, stakes, organizations, auxiliaries, and other administrative groups in the Church are sustained by common consent of the Church membership. (Read D&C 28:13.)
Application: We will pray for those who are in leadership positions over us and then work to help them fulfill their responsibilities by filling *our* responsibilities.

For additional scriptures see Topical Guide, "Covenants"; "Sustain"; "Sustaining Church Leaders."

Responsible and Accountable

48

"This life is given to prepare for the next." (Brigham Young, Journal of Discourses, *14:232.) "The most important thought I ever had was that of my individual responsibility to God." (Daniel Webster.)*

DEFINITION

To be responsible or accountable means that we are liable and answerable for our conduct and obligations, for setting goals, and for preparing ourselves to meet God.

WHY BE RESPONSIBLE AND ACCOUNTABLE?

The fact that every man is accountable to God for his own actions underlies the whole gospel plan of salvation. No one can save someone else; each must work for his own salvation, and each is responsible and accountable for what he himself does. Each person must set and work toward his own goals, prepare his own self, and accept this responsibility; only then can he be an example, a teacher for others. The second Article of Faith says, "We believe that men will be punished for their own sins, and not for Adam's transgression." "If we really desire to be saved and exalted in His [our Father's] celestial kingdom, He has told us how to proceed and has warned us that we must discharge the obligations entitling us to that exaltation. While we enjoy this blessing, it carries with it a tremendous responsibility." (George Albert Smith, general conference address, October 1940.)

PURPOSE OF THE WEEK

To understand personal responsibility in preparing to meet God, in accounting for our own self, and in goal setting, and then putting these into effect in our lives.

SUNDAY

Purpose of the day: To learn that everyone is responsible and must account to God for what he has done. (Read Romans 14:12.)

Application: We will write down why we are accountable for our actions here on this earth. Then we will read the following scriptures on preparing to meet God: Amos 4:12; D&C 1:12; D&C 78:7; Alma 12:24; Alma 34:32.

MONDAY

Purpose of the day: To learn that it is a commandment that each person must be prepared to give this accounting to God at the last days. (Read D&C 29:8.)

Application: We will talk with our family about accountability, about being prepared for the last days, and about being prepared to meet God. We will read D&C 1:12 and D&C 133:19 together.

TUESDAY

Purpose of the day: To learn that each person must be responsible for setting spiritual and temporal goals and working toward them. (Read D&C 104:13.)

Application: It is never too late to set goals and work toward achieving them. Some worthwhile goals might include (1) growing and progressing toward exaltation, (2) gaining knowledge and wisdom, (3) getting along with others and doing good for them, (4) loving God and our neighbor as ourselves, (5) obeying all of God's commandments, (6) accepting responsibility for economic efficiency, (7) accepting civil responsibility, (8) being active in building the kingdom, and (9) working toward correct attitudes. We will each write down the five most important goals in our lives. On Saturday we will check to see what progress we have made in working on them.

WEDNESDAY

Purpose of the day: To learn that each of us is responsible for taking upon himself the name of Christ. (Read 3 Nephi 27:20.)
Application: We will write down one covenant we made at baptism, and also how we take on ourselves the name of Christ when we are baptized.

THURSDAY

Purpose of the day: To learn that we are responsible and accountable to learn our duties and fulfill them. (Read D&C 107:99–100.)
Application: We will make sure that everything is in order regarding our current Church assignments.

FRIDAY

Purpose of the day: To learn that we are responsible and accountable for our own thoughts and words. (Read Matthew 12:36–37.)
Application: For this one day we will speak only the kindest words and in a tone of voice that would please our Father in heaven. Then we will try to continue this practice in the days ahead.

SATURDAY

Purpose of the day: To learn that we must not procrastinate our preparation to meet God. (Read Alma 34:33.)

Application: We will read Amos 4:12, and then promise God that we will not procrastinate our repentance and our good works. We will set a schedule to check up on how we are accomplishing our goals.

For additional scriptures see Topical Guide, "Responsibility"; "Accountability."

Testimony

49

"Inspiration, revelation to the individual soul is the rock upon which a testimony should be built and there is not one living who cannot get it if he will conform to those laws and live a clean life, which will permit the Holy Spirit to place that testimony in him." (David O. McKay, Deseret News, Church Section, *September 12, 1951, p. 4.)*

DEFINITION

A testimony is the sure knowledge, received by revelation from the Holy Ghost, of the divinity of the gospel, that Jesus is the Christ, and that a prophet heads the church.

WHY TESTIMONY?

A testimony lets us and others know that God lives, that Jesus is the Christ, that the Church is true, and that a prophet heads the Church today. A testimony helps a person live the kind of life that leads to eternal life and exaltation; it causes service and works and action. When borne, it can inspire others to service and works and action.

PURPOSE OF THE WEEK

To help us strengthen our testimonies, or to gain a testimony if we don't have one.

SUNDAY

Purpose of the day: To learn that a testimony comes through revelation from God through the power of the Holy Ghost. (Read Helaman 7:29.)

Application: We will each write our testimony on paper. Then we will read additional scriptures on testimony, especially D&C 20:26; Moroni 10:3–5; and Matthew 16:13–20.

MONDAY

Purpose of the day: To help us gain a testimony that Jesus is the Christ. (Read D&C 76:22–23.)

Application: We will discuss testimony with our family, and will bear our testimonies that Jesus is the Christ and that his church is once more upon the earth. Hymns 181, "Jesus of Nazareth, Savior and King," and 196, "Jesus, Once of Humble Birth," can help strengthen our testimonies.

TUESDAY

Purpose of the day: To learn how to gain a testimony. (Read Alma 5:45–46.)

Application: The necessary steps to gain a testimony include (1) having a desire for a testimony, (2) studying and learning the facts, (3) fasting and praying with faith in the Lord Jesus Christ, and (4) putting into practice the principles of the gospel. We will each write down a principle of the gospel about which we wish to have a stronger testimony and then go through the steps listed above to gain this testimony.

WEDNESDAY

Purpose of the day: To learn that we should not be ashamed of our testimonies, even in the face of trials and afflictions. (Read Romans 1:16.)

Application: We will resolve to always stand up for our faith and beliefs no matter what the situation.

THURSDAY

Purpose of the day: To learn that when we have a testimony, we should bear it to all the earth. (Read D&C 84:62.)
Application: We will read D&C 88:81 and then resolve to be missionaries whatever we are doing and wherever we are, and to bear our testimonies at all appropriate times.

FRIDAY

Purpose of the day: To learn that all the prophets and the scriptures have borne testimony since the beginning of time. (Read Alma 30:44.)
Application: In the latest *Conference Report* or copy of the *Ensign* that carries the general conference talks, we will read the testimony of the living prophet of the Lord.

SATURDAY

Purpose of the day: To learn that blessings come from gaining, having, and bearing a testimony. (Read D&C 62:3.)
Application: An additional reward to having our sins forgiven is the joy we gain from bringing others to repentance through our testimonies. (Read D&C 18:15–16.) We will write down two other blessings that come from having a testimony.

For additional scriptures see Topical Guide, "Testimony."

Service and Responsibilities

The Priesthood and its Functions

50

"... to hold the priesthood of God by divine authority is one of the greatest gifts that can come to a man ... " (David O. McKay, **Improvement Era,** *June 1959* *[vol. 62], p. 406.)*

DEFINITION
Priesthood is the power and authority of God by which all things are created, governed, and controlled.

WHY PRIESTHOOD AND ITS FUNCTIONS?
Without the priesthood, the work of the Lord could not go forth. If the priesthood is the power to act for the Lord, man cannot act for God without that power or authority. President David O. McKay said, "Priesthood is power and authority inherent in the Godhead. In man it is always delegated authority—it cannot be assumed with efficacy.... Whenever the Priesthood is delegated to man it is conferred upon him not as a personal distinction, although it becomes such as he

honors it, but as authority to represent Deity and an *obligation to assist* the Lord in bringing to pass the immortality and eternal life of man." (*Deseret News,* Church Section, April 20, 1935; italics added.) The Lord himself said, "And without the ordinances thereof, and the authority of the priesthood, the power of godliness is not manifest unto men in the flesh; For without this no man can see the face of God, even the Father, and live." (D&C 84:21–22.) Priesthood holders should magnify their priesthood and use it to serve the Lord and bless others.

PURPOSE OF THE WEEK

To understand the priesthood and its functions and to put this understanding to work in our daily lives.

SUNDAY

Purpose of the day: To learn that one must be called and ordained to the priesthood. (Read Alma 13:6.)

Application: If we hold the priesthood, we will trace our authority back to Christ. If we do not hold the priesthood, then we will trace the authority of our husband, brother, father, or another loved one back to Christ. Then we will see that the authority truly comes from God and not from man. (Read these additional scriptures: John 15:16; Alma 4:20; 13:3; D&C 2:1; 86:8–11.)

MONDAY

Purpose of the day: To learn that there are two priesthoods in the Church. (Read D&C 107:1.)

Application: The Lord said that the Melchizedek Priesthood holds the "right of presidency," to administer the spiritual things and the offices of the Church, the keys to spiritual blessings, receiving the mysteries, and "to enjoy the communion and presence of God the Father, and Jesus the mediator of the new covenant." (D&C 107:8, 18–19.) The lesser or Aaronic Priesthood is to administer the "outward ordinances," to hold the "keys of the ministering of angels," and to administer the "letter of the gospel." (D&C 107:14, 20.) In other words, the Lord gave two priesthoods so that the Church could be run in an orderly fashion, because he is a God of order and not of confusion. (See 1 Corinthians 14:33.) With our family, we will discuss the priesthood, its meaning, and its divisions. Hymn 20, "God of Power, God of Right," can add to the discussion.

TUESDAY

Purpose of the day: To learn that one function of the priesthood is to heal the sick. (Read James 5:14–15.)
Application: We will write down the names of those holding the priesthood whom we would call should we need to be healed (preferably family members or home teachers). Then we will decide if we have the faith to receive this blessing.

WEDNESDAY

Purpose of the day: To learn that one function of the priesthood is to bless children. (Read D&C 20:70.)
Application: Next fast Sunday, we will listen to the prayers being said when the children are blessed and think about them and what they mean.

THURSDAY

Purpose of the day: To learn that one function of the priesthood is to perform ordinations. (Read Alma 6:1.)
Application: We will list the powers given in the conferring of the Aaronic and Melchizedek priesthoods.

FRIDAY

Purpose of the day: To learn that one function of the priesthood is the giving of patriarchal blessings. (Read D&C 124:92.)
Application: Elder John A. Widtsoe of the Council of the Twelve (1872–1952) wrote: "All Church members may claim the patriarchal blessings flowing from their membership in the assemblage of families within the Church, which can be

pronounced only by men who represent the group as a whole. Therefore, patriarchs, ordained to the office, are made available in all the stakes of Zion, so that all faithful members may receive the blessings to which they are entitled." (*Evidences and Reconciliations*, Bookcraft, 1943, p. 73.) If we have not had a patriarchal blessing, we will prepare ourselves and obtain one. If we have one, we will get it out and read it, and see whether or not we are living worthy to receive the blessings set forth therein.

SATURDAY

Purpose of the day: To learn about the oath and covenant of the priesthood. (Read D&C 84:39–40.)
Application: We will read D&C 84:33–40 and ponder what this oath and covenant of the priesthood means to each of us.

For additional scriptures see Topical Guide, "Priesthood"; "Priesthood, Authority"; "Priesthood, Magnifying Callings within"; "Priesthood, Oath and Covenant."

Temple Marriage and Endowment

51

Endowed from on high with power and sealed for eternity — a gift from God for our eternal happiness.

DEFINITION
Temple marriage is a sacred relationship that binds husband and wife together with their families for eternity.

WHY TEMPLE MARRIAGE?
"Marriage, as understood by Latter-day Saints, is a covenant ordained to be everlasting. *It is the foundation for eternal exaltation, for without it there could be no eternal progress in the kingdom of God.*" (Joseph Fielding Smith, *Doctrines of Salvation,* Bookcraft, 1955, vol. 2, p. 58.) Marriage is truly a glorious responsibility: to make our relationship with our spouse one of love and spirituality that will weather the test of time and last forever. With eternal marriage comes the joy of reaching the celestial kingdom and having eternal increase of our own.

PURPOSE OF THE WEEK

To understand the endowment and temple marriage, and to strive to reach them (if we have not) or to perfect them (if we have).

SUNDAY

Purpose of the day: To learn that marriage is ordained of God. (Read D&C 49:15–16.)
Application: We will discuss with our family eternal marriage, the family, and the celestial kingdom. Hymns 294, "Love at Home," and 289, "Holy Temples on Mount Zion," can aid the discussion.

MONDAY

Purpose of the day: To learn that celestial marriage is intended by God to be a sacred, inviolable union. (Read Mark 10:9.)
Application: We will discuss the importance of commitment and fidelity in marriage.

TUESDAY

Purpose of the day: To learn that celestial marriage, along with obedience to God's laws, brings glory forever. (Read D&C 132:19.)
Application: We will write down three blessings we may receive from celestial marriage.

WEDNESDAY

Purpose of the day: To learn that we must prepare for temple marriage. (Read D&C 78:7.)
Application: Preparation for temple marriage includes physical, mental, and spiritual preparation. We will list at least five things each of us must do to prepare for temple marriage.

THURSDAY

Purpose of the day: To learn that the ordinance of endowment is necessary for temple marriage. (Read D&C 105:12.)

Application: If we have not obtained our endowments, we will start preparing to do so. If we have received them, we will go to the temple at the first opportunity. (If we do not live near a temple, we will write down the blessings received in this life from having one's endowments.)

FRIDAY

Purpose of the day: To learn that the endowment and celestial marriage must be performed in a temple of the Lord, for he has commanded his people to build houses for this purpose. (Read D&C 95:8.)

Application: We will list the things we must do in order to obtain a temple recommend. If we do not have one, we will work toward obtaining one.

SATURDAY

Purpose of the day: To learn that those who marry outside the temple but are obedient to all other commandments of God can only become angels in heaven. (Read D&C 132:15–17.)

Application: We will discuss the blessings we would lose if we were not married in the temple or if we were to break our temple covenants. Then we will vow that we will follow the commandment of the Lord about temple marriage.

For additional scriptures see Topical Guide, "Temple, House of the Lord"; "Marriage, Celestial"; "Endowment."

The Purpose of Parenthood

52

"The most important work you will do for the Church will be within the walls of your own home." (Harold B. Lee.)

WHY A PURPOSE FOR PARENTS?

Parents bring forth children and are commanded to teach them. (Read D&C 68:25f.) If they don't, how will the children learn about God? Who will teach them? Can parents abandon the responsibility for instructing their children without bringing down the wrath of God upon their heads? The scriptures say, "You have not taught your children light and truth, according to the commandments; and that wicked one hath power, as yet, over you, and this is the cause of your affliction." (D&C 93:42.) We are told to "set in order your own house, for there are many things that are not right in your house" (D&C 93:43), if we do not want to be in the power of the adversary. "No other success can compensate for failure in the home." (David O. McKay.) Failure in the home comes when we quit trying to keep the commandments.

PURPOSE OF THE WEEK

To become better parents through understanding the purpose of parenthood.

SUNDAY

Purpose of the day: To learn that parents prepare physical bodies for the spirit children of God. (Read Moses 4:22.)
Application: One of the main purposes for coming to earth is to receive a body. "The man, and the woman who are the agents, in the providence of God, to bring living souls into the world, are made before God and the heavens, as responsible for these acts as is God himself responsible for the works of his own hands...." (Joseph F. Smith, *Gospel Doctrine*, Deseret Book, 1973, p. 273.) We will thank God for the opportunity to be or to become a parent. (Read the conference address by Bishop H. Burke Peterson in the January 1973 *Ensign.*)

MONDAY

Purpose of the day: To learn that parents are to provide for they physical needs of their children. (Read Mosiah 4:14.)
Application: With our family, we will discuss the purpose of parents bringing children into the world and caring for them physically, emotionally, and spiritually. Hymn 96, "Dearest Children, God Is Near You," can aid the discussion.

TUESDAY

Purpose of the day: To learn that parents are commanded to bring up their children in light and truth. (Read D&C 93:40 and Proverbs 22:6.)
Application: We will make a teaching opportunity to teach one gospel truth each day this week.

WEDNESDAY

Purpose of the day: To learn that teaching our children includes teaching faith, repentance, baptism, and the gift of the Holy Ghost. (Read D&C 68:25.)

Application: We will discuss with our family the principle that shows that faith, repentance, baptism, and the gift of the Holy Ghost are all given to us because of Jesus Christ.

THURSDAY

Purpose of the day: To learn that teaching our children includes teaching them to pray and to walk uprightly before the Lord. (Read D&C 68:28.)

Application: We will read Matthew 7:7–8 to our children and discuss this scripture with them. We will remind them of this scripture in regard to individual and family prayer.

FRIDAY

Purpose of the day: To learn that teaching our children includes teaching love and service to others. (Read Mosiah 4: 14–15.)

Application: When one is a loving person, he is full of service to others and does not say one cross or unkind word. For one day, we will concentrate on being completely kind and loving and will say no cross or unkind words to anyone. We will live this one day as if Christ were right by our side.

SATURDAY

Purpose of the day: To learn that parenthood is a full-time responsibility, and failure occurs when we quit trying. (Read Deuteronomy 6:7.)

Application: We will renew our commitment to God that we will truly accept and fulfill the responsibilities of parenthood while here on the earth.

For additional scriptures see Topical Guide, all topics on "Family."

Family Responsibilities
53

The basic unit of the Church is the family. The divine family of Christ will be comprised of righteous families. Our goal is to build strong families through the gospel of Jesus Christ.

WHY FAMILY RESPONSIBILITIES?

A home is not merely a place to refuel and/or rest. It is a place where a family works, loves, cries, and laughs together, where family members share with one another. Families that accept the responsibility to love and help each other will remain united. Families that do not will become estranged from each other. President David O. McKay said, "I regard it as an incontrovertible fact that in no marriage circle can true peace, love, purity, chastity, and happiness be found, in which is not present the spirit of Christ.... God help us to build homes in which the spirit of heaven on earth may be experienced." (General priesthood meeting, April 5, 1952.)

PURPOSE OF THE WEEK

To learn what family responsibilities are and to begin to accept and fulfill them.

SUNDAY

Purpose of the day: To learn that one family responsibility is to strengthen love in the home. (Read Jacob 3:7.)

Application: President David O. McKay stated that "homes are made permanent through love." (*Pathways to Happiness*, Bookcraft, 1957, p. 114.) We will each do something special for every member of the family to show them that we love them. We will also write a note of love and appreciation for each of them. (Read Mosiah 4:15; D&C 20:47, 51.)

MONDAY

Purpose of the day: To learn that one family responsibility is to hold family home evening. (Read Moses 6:58.)

Application: We will discuss with our family the purpose of family home evening. Hymn 294, "Love at Home," can assist in the discussion.

TUESDAY

Purpose of the day: To learn that one family responsibility is to do genealogy work. (Read D&C 2:2.)

Application: Genealogy is more than proxy work. It is a family concern, the patriarchal order, and includes appreciation for those who have gone before and those yet to come. We will take a picture of our family and put it with our family record. We will write on the back of the photo an interesting story about this particular time.

WEDNESDAY

Purpose of the day: To learn that one family responsibility is to pray together. (Read 3 Nephi 18:21.)

Application: We will make a special effort to hold family prayer night and morning from this day on.

THURSDAY

Purpose of the day: To learn that one family responsibility is to learn to respect and obey laws. (Read D&C 134:1, 5.)

Application: "We cannot be in rebellion against the law and be in harmony with the Lord, for he has commanded us to 'be subject to the powers that be, until he reigns whose right it is to reign....' (D&C 58:22.)" (Joseph Fielding Smith, general priesthood meeting, April 1971.) We will read and discuss with our family the 12th Article of Faith.

FRIDAY

Purpose of the day: To learn that one family responsibility is to work together. (Read D&C 68:31.)
Application: We will make a chart showing the division of work in our family and what each person does. We will note how every member is necessary and needed for a happy family.

SATURDAY

Purpose of the day: To learn that obedience to parents is based on love and trust. (Read Ephesians 6:1–3.)
Application: We will determine whether our children are obedient because they love and trust us or because they are afraid of us.

For additional scriptures see Topical Guide, all topics on "Family."

Doing Temple Work

54

"There must be this chain in the holy Priesthood; it must be welded together from the latest generation that lives on the earth back to Father Adam, to bring back all that can be saved and placed where they can receive salvation and glory in some kingdom. This Priesthood has to do it; this Priesthood is for this purpose...." (Brigham Young, Discourses of Brigham Young, *Deseret Book, 1946, p. 407.)*

DEFINITION

Temple work by proxy is that process whereby families are sealed together for all eternity.

WHY TEMPLE WORK?

The Lord loves all his children, not just those who have joined his church today, and he wants them all, including those who did not have a chance to hear the gospel while living on the earth, to have the chance to return and live with him in the celestial kingdom. Therefore, temple work in The Church of Jesus Christ of Latter-day Saints means everyone has a personal responsibility to gather the names of his direct ancestors and have the temple work done for them, so that all members of a family can be sealed together.

PURPOSE OF THE WEEK

To learn about and begin doing the temple work for our ancestors.

SUNDAY

Purpose of the day: To learn that everyone is to be judged by God for his own works, out of the books and records kept on earth and in heaven. (Read Revelation 20:12.)

Application: We will fill out a family group sheet for our own immediate family, which is a beginning of the record we will make. (Read these scriptures also: D&C 1:8; 85:3–12; Moses 6:5; Malachi 3:1; 4:1.)

MONDAY

Purpose of the day: To learn that what is bound or recorded on earth is also bound or recorded in heaven. (Read D&C 127:7.)

Application: We will discuss with our family proxy work in the temple and why it is important for and to them. Hymns 289, "Holy Temples on Mount Zion," and 288, "How Beautiful Thy Temples, Lord," can add to the discussion.

TUESDAY

Purpose of the day: To learn that temple work will link families together for eternity. (Read D&C 128:15.)

Application: We will fill out family group sheets for the generation just prior to our own immediate family.

WEDNESDAY

Purpose of the day: To learn that temple work provides a way of salvation for those who did not have the chance to accept the gospel while living on the earth. (Read D&C 128:5.)

Application: Missionaries are teaching those in the spirit world who died without being able to hear the gospel on earth. Temple ordinances performed by proxies provide salvation for these people. We will read 1 Peter 3:19–20 about Christ preaching to the spirits in prison.

THURSDAY

Purpose of the day: To learn that each of us has a *personal responsibility* for our own dead; we are all to be saviors on Mount Zion. (Read D&C 127:6 and Obadiah 1:21.)
Application: We will begin to find out what research and temple work has been done on our family lines and then formulate a plan of research to go from there.

FRIDAY

Purpose of the day: To learn that Elijah returned the keys of this work to the earth, as was prophesied. (Read D&C 2:1–3.)
Application: We will read D&C 110:13–16 about Elijah actually returning the keys. Then we will each write one letter to someone, seeking genealogical information.

SATURDAY

Purpose of the day: To learn that genealogy is a family duty, not just something to be done when we are old. (Read D&C 20:47, 51.)
Application: We will determine how family members can turn their hearts to their fathers or children through making personal histories, reading histories of those gone on, and learning appreciation for those gone on.

For additional scriptures see Topical Guide, "Genealogy and Temple Work"; "Salvation for the Dead."

Tithes and Offerings
55

The Lord has commanded us to pay tithes and offerings for the purpose of building the kingdom.

DEFINITION
Tithing is paying one-tenth of a person's yearly increase, profit, intake, industry, etc., either in money or in kind to the Church.

WHY TITHES AND OFFERINGS?
"There is no such thing as an organization of men for any purpose of importance, without provisions for carrying out its designs. The law of tithing is the law of revenue for the Church of Jesus Christ of Latter-day Saints. Without it, it would be impossible to carry on the purposes of the Lord." (Joseph F. Smith, *Gospel Doctrine,* Deseret Book, 1973, p. 226.) The Lord needs the tithes and offerings of his church members to help run his church, to help the poor, to build temples and chapels, and to help build the Church on earth. In addition to this purpose, personal benefits are also derived by individuals who pay their tithes and offerings. These include showing love through service to the Lord, protection from condemnation,

gaining spirituality or power to become closer to the Lord, acquiring self-control through learning to subdue wants and desires, and learning to budget personal income.

PURPOSE OF THE WEEK

To pay our tithes and offerings to the Lord with a good attitude and knowledge as to why we do it.

SUNDAY

Purpose of the day: To learn that tithing means to give one-tenth of our increase to the Lord. (Read D&C 119:4.)
Application: We will answer these questions: Do we pay our tithing? Do we give the Lord his share? If so, why? If not, why? We will read these scriptures on tithing: Acts 20:35; 2 Corinthians 9:6–7; Alma 13:15; D&C 19:26; D&C 120:1.

MONDAY

Purpose of the day: To learn that payment of tithes and offerings is a sacrifice required of the Lord. (Read D&C 97:12.)
Application: We will discuss with our family the payment of tithes and offerings. If we have not done so already, we will set up tithing boxes or bottles for each of the children so they may pay their tithing. If necessary, we will make a chart to help the family learn about tithing. We will also discuss the blessings that can come to our family from the payment of tithing. Hymn 218, "We Give Thee But Thine Own," can assist the discussion.

TUESDAY

Purpose of the day: To learn that the law of tithing has been on the earth since its beginning. (Read Genesis 14:20.)
Application: We will list reasons why we think that tithing has been necessary to people since the beginning of mankind on the earth.

WEDNESDAY

Purpose of the day: To learn the answer to the question, Can a man rob God? (Read Malachi 3:8–9 and 3 Nephi 24:8–9.)
Application: We will list what problems on the earth today we think are being caused because people do not pay tithing. We will also make a commitment to the Lord that we will always pay our tithes and offerings.

THURSDAY

Purpose of the day: To learn of the offerings Latter-day Saints should pay in addition to tithing. (Read D&C 124:75.)
Application: We will make a list of the offerings we are asked to pay in our ward or branch. Then we will answer these two questions: How do we stand? How will the Lord view us and our contributions?

FRIDAY

Purpose of the day: To learn that those who pay their obligations to the Lord will "not be burned" at the day of judgment. (Read D&C 64:23.)
Application: We will read D&C 85:3 and commit ourselves to be full tithe payers.

SATURDAY

Purpose of the day: To learn of the blessings that come from payment of tithes and offerings. (Read Malachi 3:10 and 3 Nephi 24:10.)
Application: We will list several blessings we have already received from payment of tithes and offerings.

For additional scriptures see Topical Guide, "Tithing"; "Offering."

Missionary Work
56

"This is the appointed time for the preaching of the gospel in all the world and for the building up of the Lord's kingdom in every nation." (Joseph Fielding Smith, general conference address, October 1971.) "Above all, teach the gospel of Jesus Christ with power and authority and continue to bear witness to the divine mission of our Lord and Master, Jesus Christ." (Harold B. Lee, general conference address, October 1971.)

DEFINITION

Missionary work means being engaged in any manner (i.e., finding, friendshipping, teaching, preaching, using example) of bringing the gospel of Jesus Christ to all the world.

WHY MISSIONARY WORK?

"There is no work that any of us can engage in that is as important as preaching the gospel and building up the Church and kingdom of God on earth." (Joseph Fielding Smith, general conference address, April 1972.) Because there are many people on the earth who do not yet have a knowledge of the truth (D&C 123:12), and because the Lord wants all his children to learn of him so that they might not perish in unbelief (Mosiah 28:3), missionaries are sent as instruments in the hands of the Lord to bring the message of truth and salvation to his children (Alma 29:9).

PURPOSE OF THE WEEK

To understand missionary work and to become missionaries in our own everyday lives.

SUNDAY

Purpose of the day: To learn that the world is ready and waiting for the missionaries. (Read D&C 4:4.)
Application: We will make a commitment that we will help the Lord with his missionary work. We will read these scriptures on missionary work: Isaiah 61:1–3; Matthew 4:16, 23; Mosiah 28:3; Alma 29:9–10; D&C 18:10; D&C 123:12.

MONDAY

Purpose of the day: To prepare ourselves to be missionaries. (Read D&C 112:28.)
Application: We will discuss with our family how we can prepare to be missionaries every day. We will also start a missionary fund jar for the children in the family, where extra change is put aside for a mission. Hymn 249, "Called to Serve," can reinforce this discussion.

TUESDAY

Purpose of the day: To learn that the power of the word of God is manifest by the missionaries. (Read Alma 31:5.)
Application: The power of the word of God is the power to do good and to follow the commandments of the Lord. Missionary work brings with it this power to do good and cause others to do so also. We will write down how the power of

the word of God can affect us in being missionaries through example and word of mouth.

WEDNESDAY

Purpose of the day: To learn that missionaries are to go to the whole world, two by two. (Read Mormon 9:22 and D&C 52:10.)

Application: We will write a letter to a missionary from our ward or branch to thank him for his service to the Lord and to encourage him to continue in this service.

THURSDAY

Purpose of the day: To learn that missionaries are to cry repentance to the world. (Read Alma 5:49–50.)

Application: We will read the following scriptures in which the Lord has said missionaries must cry repentance to the people: Alma 5:51; Alma 13:21; Ether 11:20; D&C 18:14–15; D&C 34:6.

FRIDAY

Purpose of the day: To learn that every member of the Church is a missionary, and we are to share the gospel of Jesus Christ. (Read D&C 88:81.)

Application: Through prayer, we will select a person or family with whom we can share the gospel.

SATURDAY

Purpose of the day: To learn of the joys and blessings that come from missionary work. (Read D&C 84:80.)

Application: The blessings promised of the Lord for doing missionary work include joy and rejoicing with those souls whom we have helped (D&C 18:15–16), our testimonies recorded in heaven (D&C 62:3), our tongues loosened so that we might really preach the gospel (D&C 31:3; Moses 6:32), and the continued presence of the Comforter (D&C 42:16–

17; 50:14, 17). We will each list the blessing we would especially like for preaching the gospel.

For additional scriptures see Topical Guide, "Missionary Work."

The Sabbath Day

57

"The Sabbath is not just another day on which we merely rest from work, free to spend it as our light-mindedness may suggest. It is a holy day, the Lord's day, to be spent as a day of worship and reverence." (The First Presidency, June 20, 1959.)

DEFINITION

The Sabbath day is the one day in seven when we rest from our labors and worship our God.

WHY THE SABBATH DAY?

The Lord has given his children one day in seven whereby they may rest from their labors and devote time to him and his work. He has asked them to observe the Sabbath day and keep it holy. (D&C 68:29.) But many people do not keep this commandment. To our Heavenly Father it is one of the principal commandments. It is a test to see if we will do all things commanded of us. This commandment is being broken more and more each year. It behooves the children of God to keep this commandment, or they will receive the condemnation of the Lord.

PURPOSE OF THE WEEK
To keep the Sabbath day holy always.

SUNDAY
Purpose of the day: To learn that the Lord has commanded his children to keep the Sabbath day holy. (Read Deuteronomy 5:15.)
Application: In this scripture, God has specifically stated that keeping the Sabbath day is a commandment. More than twenty different instances are recorded in the scriptures in which the Lord has said we are to observe and keep the Sabbath day holy. We will make a list of the many things one can and should do on the Sabbath day. We will also read these scriptures pertaining to this commandment: Mark 2:27; Mosiah 13:16; Mosiah 18:23; D&C 59:10–13.

MONDAY
Purpose of the day: To learn that we are to work six days and rest on the seventh. (Read Exodus 20:9–10; Mosiah 13:17–18; Deuteronomy 5:13–14.)
Application: With our family, we will discuss keeping the Sabbath day holy and working on the other six days. Hymns 146, "Gently Raise the Sacred Strain," and 276, "Come Away to the Sunday School," can aid the discussion.

TUESDAY
Purpose of the day: To learn that observance of the Sabbath was instituted following God's creation of the earth. (Read Genesis 2:1–3; Mosiah 13:19.)
Application: After reading the scriptures suggested, we will write down what "sanctified" and "hallowed" mean. Then we will think of those things that will sanctify and hallow the Sabbath day.

WEDNESDAY

Purpose of the day: To learn that when we keep the Sabbath day, we are making and keeping a covenant with the Lord. (Read Exodus 31:13, 16.)

Application: We will write down the covenant made between ourselves and the Lord that we make and try to keep each Sabbath day.

THURSDAY

Purpose of the day: To learn that we are to offer our sacraments on the Lord's day to keep ourselves clean from worldly sins. (Read D&C 59:9–10.)

Application: Each person must offer up his sacraments—"a broken heart and a contrite spirit" (D&C 59:8)—before he can keep himself free from sin. If we devote ourselves to the Lord and give him our offering of a broken heart and contrite spirit, we can keep the Sabbath day holy and help keep ourselves from sinning. We will write down how keeping the Sabbath day can help us resist temptation.

FRIDAY

Purpose of the day: To learn that Christ is the Lord of the Sabbath. (Read Mark 2:28.)

Application: We will make a commitment that next Sunday we will spend the day as if Christ were physically present with us during the whole day. We will make our day one in which Christ would be happy to be present with us.

SATURDAY

Purpose of the day: To learn of the blessings that come from observing the Sabbath day. (Read D&C 59:12–18.)

Application: We will read Isaiah 58:13–14 for further blessings that come from observing the Sabbath day. Then we will list those blessings we have already received and those that we want to receive by keeping the Sabbath day holy.

For additional scriptures see Topical Guide, "Sabbath."

Worship and Meditation

58

"Our responsibility in the Church is to worship the Lord in spirit and in truth, and this we are seeking to do with all heart, might, and mind." (Joseph Fielding Smith, general conference address, October 1971.) "Meditation is one of the most secret, most sacred doors through which we pass into the presence of the Lord." (David O. McKay, general conference address, April 1946.)

DEFINITION

Worship is giving honor, courtesy, devotion, respect and reverence to God. *Meditation* is deep thinking and continued reflection; it may include private devotion.

WHY WORSHIP AND MEDITATE?

The Lord has commanded men to worship God; "and him only shalt thou serve." (Luke 4:8.) True worship means to honor and revere the Lord God in the name of his Son, Jesus Christ. It also means being obedient to the commandments and laws given by the Lord for the benefit of man and meditating upon them.

PURPOSE OF THE WEEK
To learn the nature of true worship and meditation.

SUNDAY
Purpose of the day: To learn that men are commanded to worship God. (Read Matthew 4:10.)
Application: President Joseph Fielding Smith said, "The supreme act of worship is to keep the commandments, to follow in the footsteps of the Son of God, to do ever those things that please him. It is one thing to give lip service to the Lord; it is quite another to respect and honor his will by following the example he has set for us." (General conference address, October 1971.) We will write down at least three ways in which we regularly worship the Lord. We will also read several scriptures about worshiping the Lord, including Psalm 95:6–7; Luke 4:8; John 4:22–26; 1 Nephi 17:55; D&C 20:19; and D&C 93:19.

MONDAY
Purpose of the day: To learn about how we should worship. (Read 2 Nephi 25:29.)
Application: We will each commit ourselves to worship the Lord with all our heart, might, mind, strength, and soul, and will discuss this with our family. Hymn 76, "God of Our Fathers, We Come unto Thee," can be of benefit in the discussion.

TUESDAY
Purpose of the day: To learn that the Saints are to meet together at least once a week to worship God. (Read Mosiah 18:25.)
Application: We will decide that from now on we will attend church with an attitude of wanting to give and learn from it and because we love God.

WEDNESDAY

Purpose of the day: To learn that our meetings are to be conducted through the Spirit of the Lord. (Read Moroni 6:9.)
Application: Knowing that having the Spirit is vital to worship, we will strive always to have it with us when we worship.

THURSDAY

Purpose of the day: To learn that worship includes meditation. (Read 3 Nephi 17:3.)
Application: We will commit ourselves to meditate and ponder upon the things of God as a way of worshiping him.

FRIDAY

Purpose of the day: To practice meditating during the day and at night. (Read Joshua 1:8.)
Application: We will begin spending five to fifteen minutes daily in meditating and pondering on the ways, words, and works of the Lord.

SATURDAY

Purpose of the day: To meditate for our own profit. (Read 1 Timothy 4:15–16.)
Application: Meditation on the things of the Lord is for our own benefit. We will write out two or more ways in which we will benefit from meditating on the things of God. (Reread Joshua 1:8 to see what the Lord has said here about profiting from meditation.)

For additional scriptures see Topical Guide, "Worship"; "Ponder"; "Meditation."

Observing Special Occasions

It is not intended that the chapters in this book need be studied and considered consecutively. If a family has a particular problem, need, or interest in a special subject, the time to consider that subject is now, not according to a preset schedule. In like manner, no matter where a family begins its study of the scriptures, special holidays and occasions may indicate that a particular chapter is desirable for that time. For example, the following subjects may be considered during the weeks of holidays and other special family happenings.

New Year's Day: No. 7, "Goal Setting."

Valentine's Day: No. 29, "Love."

Easter: No. 23, "Jesus Christ, Our Savior"; No. 25, "Atonement"; No. 27, "Resurrection and Judgment"; No. 28, "Our Ultimate Goal: Exaltation."

Memorial Day: No. 30, "Sacrifice," and No. 40, "Loyalty."

Thanksgiving: No. 32, "Gratitude."

Christmas: No. 23, "Jesus Christ, Our Savior," and No. 24, "Jesus Said, 'Come Follow Me.'"

A Missionary Call: No. 56, "Missionary Work."

A Baptism: No 13, "Baptism," and No. 14, "Receiving the Holy Ghost."

A Death in the Family: No. 28, "Our Ultimate Goal: Exaltation," and No. 54, "Doing Temple Work."

Index

Accountability, 157
Atonement, 83
Attitude, 117

Backbiting, 147
Baptism, 43
Book of Mormon, 13
Born again—true conversion, 49

Chastity, 144
"Come, follow me," 80
Contention, 147
Conversion, true, 49
Courage, 120
Courtesy and manners, 123
Covenant making, 154
Criticism, 151

Diligence, 120

Endowment, temple, 171
Endurance, 120
Envy, 147
Exaltation, 93

Faith, power and use of, 27; in Jesus Christ, 30; in God, 33
Fall, the, 67
Family responsibilities, 177
Fasting, 6
Forgiveness, 40

Goal setting, 22; ultimate: exaltation, 93
God, faith in, 33; is all-powerful, 61; of love, mercy, justice, 64
Gratitude, 108

Habits and traditions, 114
Holidays, 196
Holy Ghost, receiving the, 46; how to keep, 52
Humility, 126

Integrity and sincerity, 129

Jesus Christ, faith in, 30; our Savior, 77; following, 80
Journals, records and, 19
Judging, 151
Justice, 64

Kindness, 111

Leaders, sustaining, 154
Love, 64, 99
Loyalty, 132

Manners, courtesy and, 123
Marriage, temple, 171
Meditation, worship and, 193
Mercy, 64
Missionary work, 186
Modesty, 144

Obedience, 105
Offerings, tithes and, 183

Parenthood, purpose of, 174
Patience, 141
Plan of salvation, 73
Prayer, 3
Priesthood and its functions, 167

Records and journals, 19
Repentance, 37
Responsibilities, family, 177
Responsibility, 157
Resurrection and judgment, 89
Revelation, 55

Sabbath day, 190
Sacrament, 86
Sacrifice, 102
Salvation, plan of, 73
Scriptures, searching, 16
Self-control, 135
Self-esteem, 138
Selfishness, 147

Sincerity, integrity and, 129
Special occasions, 196
Standard works, 9
Strife, 147
Sustaining leaders, 154

Temple marriage and endowment, 171
Temple work, 180
Temptations, 70
Testimony, 161

Tithes and offerings, 183
Tolerance, 141
Traditions, habits and, 114

Ultimate goal: exaltation, 93

Value of standard works, 9
Virtue, 144

Worship and meditation, 193